Angels Everwatching

One family's testimony
of God's protection
and mercy

**Robert, Rosemarie,
Timothy & Amy Baghurst**

The right of Robert Baghurst, Rosemarie Baghurst,
Timothy Baghurst, and Amy Baghurst to be identified as
the authors of this work has been asserted in accordance
with the Copyright, Designs and Patents Act 1988.

© Robert Baghurst, Rosemarie Baghurst,
Timothy Baghurst, and Amy Baghurst 2005

First published 2005

ISBN 1-905447-00-0

Twoedged Sword Publications
PO Box 266, Waterlooville, PO7 5ZT
www.twoedgedswordpublications.co.uk

The Baghurst Family

Robert & Rosemarie

Timothy

Amy

Introduction

We've often been asked if the story of our time in Liberia has ever been written down, but alas, not one of us has endeavoured to complete this mammoth task. We've made tapes and notes, recounted the story countless times, but never taken the initiative to actually document the events that took place at the end of October 1992.

Having written some stories now for our grandchildren I (Rosemarie) was encouraged to record this account as yet another story to add to their collection. At the same time, our son Timothy decided it was time we wrote the story of our experiences in Liberia. This was more than mere coincidence, and since Robert and I were both at home with malaria it seemed an excellent time to begin.

We have written this book, therefore, as a family venture where I transcribed Robert's dictation as well as my own, with Timothy writing his story from the perspective of a young teenager and adding a whole new dimension to what happened.

It is not a thrilling story, but as accurate a record as we can remember that extols our Lord, and His grace, mercy and loving protection in what was potentially an incident of international proportions.

In the writing process it has become evident that we were more than once alerted to the fact of God's divine protection and also His angels being ever present with us. I'm quite sure we will never see angels manifested in this life in all their glory and splendour, nor do I desire to since reading John's, Ezekiel's or Daniel's accounts of them, but they are messengers from God and spiritual beings that we take all too much for granted. It is therefore good to recall that He does have "His Angels Ever Watching" over us.

Having just found some of my old notes from Liberia I have been interested to read of the contrasts I had made between the childhoods of our own children and of those amongst whom we lived. We are born, for example, in a nice hospital bed with the best medical care and good hygienic facilities, about which we would soon complain if they were lacking. If we need emergency care it is there, including oxygen and incubators. Our friends in Liberia, however, are born on a dirt floor in a mud hut and left quite alone until the placenta is also delivered, and even then the child is not really considered a person until he or she can walk behind his or her mother and call her name. Hence if they do die at birth or in infancy not too many tears are shed and the child is buried in a termite hill so it can be eaten well enough (by the "bug-a-bugs") so as not to return again.

All we have to do in our western world is to enjoy our newborn child. However, for Liberians there are the many superstitions, putting the bloody blade on the baby's forehead a certain number of times, not taking the babe outside for a certain number of days, having witnesses to the burial of the placenta in a defined manner, the presentation of the child….It would take a whole volume to recount these many traditions, including all the situations in which, interestingly, the number 3 is used for a woman and number 4 for a man.

Our childhood is an enjoyable one of play and schooling when of a sufficient age. Here the child is often left with its grandmother or other female relative on whom it may suckle when hungry. Then, growing up, it is not long before children are carrying small tins of water on their heads or even younger siblings on their backs. They learn to cut wood and from an early age, to chase the birds from their rice farms and other such tasks within their ability. Their playtime consists of fishing, catching small animals to roast and hunting with a slingshot (known to them as "rubber gun"). Schooling is rare, or nonexistent, especially for girls.

As a child I was brought up under the sound of the gospel whereby from my early years I understood and believed in the death, burial and resurrection of Jesus Christ for my salvation. Many in Liberia have heard the name of Jesus Christ, but have no idea who exactly He is, and even less what He has done in His great love for them.

Liberia's motto has always intrigued me, as it states, "For the Love of Liberty brought us here." It has always been their boast to be the first African nation that was free, all the others having first been colonised. Actually this has been to their disadvantage since they had no strong Western influence to educate, support, and give them a good basis from which to work and grow. To the contrary, they have always been a poor nation, proud to be free, but wholly enslaved to the animistic traditions which they tenaciously hold.

Again, the contrast is striking when compared to the rich wealth of the more developed countries in the western world. True riches and freedom, however, are found only in Christ our Lord. How we long to see those of West Africa brought under not just the sound, but also the true understanding of the truth of His Word and plan of salvation for a lost world! We who are free in Christ may live to serve Him who died for us and rose again. It is our prayer that in our doing so He will be pleased to use us to the saving of many of these dear and precious souls to the glory of His name.

A Brief History of the Baghurst Family and the 1990's War in Liberia

"Mrs. Finch, your daughter is hanging from a tree in the garden; it seems she is caught up there by her dress." Well, I, Rosemarie, must have been two or three and from that time was dressed in trousers like my elder brothers. Hence I grew up as a tomboy, always regretting I was the little girl my parents had longed for – until my teenage years when adolescence kicked in….

When I first saw Robert in a small chapel in Derbyshire, England, I instantly knew he was the answer to my specific prayers for a husband. However, the second week, when he came with his cousin, who wore a wedding ring, I told God that He had made a big mistake! Of course it was I who was mistaken and after a two-and-half year courtship we were married in that little church. Ten years and three children later (of which one, a son, died), God challenged us from Romans 12:1-2 to give our lives entirely to Him. At this same time we were invited to attend Bible school with New Tribes Mission in Matlock, England, and thus began a process that led us out to the foreign field of Liberia on October 3, 1985.

After four months of orientation at our main base in Tugbaken (a new base was being built a mile away on a hill and thus called by the local people Biwiken) we were asked to join the team working amongst the Tajuoson (*tie-you-sown*) ethnic group in Sinoe County, just 190 miles north—almost halfway to the capital of Monrovia. Thus it was that on Valentine's Day, 1986, we left our two small children in Tugbaken (Amy, age 10, and Timothy 6), to commence the arduous task of reaching this people group with the gospel of Christ in their very own language.

Amy and Timothy first lived with two families, and

then in a family-style dormitory over the next five years, travelling to spend all their school breaks with us.

We were able to leave Liberia at the end of May 1990, a week earlier than planned, but just before the international airport was blown up. Our furlough was extended an extra year due to the warfare, but also to accommodate for Amy's schooling, and to spend time with my mother who was terminally ill. Robert spent three months back in Liberia from March-June 1992 and then Robert, Timothy and I returned to West Africa in August, leaving Amy in England with a caring Christian family. We then left Timothy in a family-style dormitory, set up for the children of those from the Liberian mission field, in Yamoussoukro, Ivory Coast. Robert and I then journeyed back into Liberia crossing the Cavalla River which marks the border between the two countries.

Fairly unexpectedly to most, the Liberian civil war erupted in December 1989 when a group of rebels to the government, calling themselves the National Patriotic Front of Liberia (NPFL), invaded the country from the Ivory Coast. They were led by Charles Taylor with the aid of troops from other nations and the support of two ethnic groups, the Mano and Gio, who all held grudges against the current President Doe regime and his ten year dictatorship over the country.

Because Liberia has never been under colonial rule, many times in its history the presidents have become dictators, grabbing whatever power and money is available before either being run out of the country to live a life of luxury elsewhere or the inevitable *coup d'état*. These changes occurred frequently, mainly due to the inappropriate use of power. It has been often the case that presidents bestow particular favour and power upon those originating from their own tribe or ethnic group, and in so doing cause much dissension and anger amongst other groups who have not been given the same treatment.

The entrance of Taylor was Christmas Eve 1989 and he made his way steadily across the country recruiting troops from those dissatisfied with the government or by drugs etc. They went looting, burning, raping and killing along the way and took the Buchanan port. Doe would deny their success, but we knew it was true via other missions on the radio. They went south, down country, around July 1990 and Doe was killed in September. The whole thing was bloody and many villages even wiped completely out of existence.

The NPFL was split in early 1990 when Prince Johnson formed his own rebel force, which he decided to call the Independent National Patriotic Front, or INPFL. The INPFL and in particular Prince Johnson were to become notorious for their savagry, and often forces opposing him would cut and run before the inevitable massacre. Another faction had also emerged from the fighting, calling themselves the Armed Forces of Liberia (AFL).

August 1990 brought about a coalition of West African countries which were concerned about the situation in Liberia. They formed the monitoring group ECOMOG or ECOWAS in order to help ensure that the country did not descend into chaos.

In order to attempt to stabilise the country by installing an interim government, ECOMOG convened a meeting of Liberian political leaders. NPFL leader Charles Taylor refused to attend and it was decided that Dr. Amos Sawyer, a political science professor at the University of Liberia, was to be elected President of the "Interim Government of National Unity" (IGNU).

One month later saw the capture of President Doe by INPFL rebels as he attempted to meet with ECOMOG officials. Doe was tortured and executed (on videotape, no less) by the now notorious Prince Johnson.

Following the execution of Doe, things rapidly began to fall apart. More factions emerged, such as the United Liberation Movement of Liberia for Democracy or ULIMO. This faction also followed the tradition of the previous groups by continuing the rape and pillage of the country.

While Johnson and his INPFL controlled the capital, Monrovia, Taylor and his NPFL controlled most of the countryside. This continued to cause much suffering for the innocent citizens caught in between. A village might be flying the flag of one particular faction that was dominant in the area, but as soon as this faction lost ground, the new faction entering the village would execute a select few for flying the opposition's flag and replace it with their own. When they lost ground once again, the former or yet another faction entering the village would carry out the same executions for flying the opposition's flag, thus creating a never-ending circle of persecution.

The end of October 1991, however, saw a meeting in Yamoussoukro, the political capital of the Ivory Coast, of six heads of states along with Dr. Amos Sawyer of the IGNU and Charles Taylor of the NPFL. From this series of meetings came the creation of the Yamoussoukro IV Accord, which called for a supervised ceasefire by ECOMOG and the encampment of all rebel forces.

The Yamoussoukro IV Accord lasted until October 1992, when the NPFL broke the accord by rearming and once again assaulting the city of Monrovia. It is at this point that our personal story begins…

CHAPTER ONE

All Change   October 1992

Rosemarie

How can things change so rapidly? Yet change they did. One day there was talk of "skirmishes in the country" and the next a major escalation in the fighting was headed towards Monrovia, the capital city of Liberia. We had felt pretty safe down country, right down in the southern corner. In fact, we were so far removed from any such activity that we were attempting to reestablish our main mission base at Biwiken after rebels had usurped it for their headquarters a couple of years earlier. Some of our missionary men had been living there for the last nine months with their wives joining them for the final four months. It had seemed so comparatively safe, and yes, the "boys at the gates" were generally a pain, but then it has always been that way in Liberia—and it was just a part of life there….

Homeward Bound   October 10

Timothy

Life was pretty idyllic for a lad of 13 coming up to the October half-term break at school. Okay, so my grades were not that hot in algebra, but the more important aspects of life for a young male teenager (predominantly sports) far outweighed the negative ones of a couple of bad grades. In addition to that fact was the excitement and liberation of returning from England to Liberia, which I had not seen for two years now. On reflection, I suppose living the life I had in Ivory Coast at the dorm for mission kids wasn't all that bad, but nothing could compare to returning to a place where I had spent my childhood. I was finally going home!

As my school was based at Yamoussoukro, which was located in the middle of Ivory Coast, the first stage of our trip took us down to Tabou where we spent the night just an hour or so from the border crossing into Liberia. There were quite a few of us going across for the two-week break. The MK's (Mission Kids) besides me were the three Richardsons, (Laura, Mary and Brian). Arnie Johnson, son of my dorm parents, came along as a friend.

In order to enter Liberia we had to traverse the Cavalla River, the natural border between Liberia and Ivory Coast, by barge. While crossing we were given the continual warnings about being respectful to all the rebels and not speaking unless spoken to. Personally, I couldn't wait to start practicing my Liberian English.

Now, anyone who has experienced losing something that they cherished, only to find it later, would understand to some degree how I felt stepping off that barge onto Liberian soil. There before me lay a constant expanse of dense, green jungle, broken only by a small, heavily rutted dirt road leading off into the bush. I had grown up in Liberia, spending five years hunting in the jungle, fishing in the rivers, building forts, growing fruit, and pretty much anything else that an imaginative kid could devise. So for me the vision now before me brought back all those memories that had receded for two years in a Western world where none of my friends at school could even begin to understand....

The trip to Biwiken, our main base in Liberia, was pretty much uneventful except for the novelty of seeing and passing through the checkpoints. Naturally I couldn't keep my mouth shut and ended up having quite a conversation in Liberian English with one of the rebels. (I was particularly surprised, and somewhat proud, it must be said, at how quickly it all came back to me.) After a couple of hours we had bounced and jolted our way to Biwiken.

Rosemarie

Back at Biwiken, you could say that I was pretty excited. In the same way that I cannot explain the love I had first meeting Robert so I cannot explain how I fell in love with the country of Liberia. Indeed there are many reasons why I should *not* love this country, as the temperature often soars into the hundreds; you are soaked with perspiration from morning until night, not to mention the dirt and disease associated with village life in the tropics.

It's amazing when I think back to all the reasons why I should not have come to Africa, one of the main ones being my paranoia about spiders since a nasty experience as a child. I never have learnt to live with them. They move so fast and in fact there they are not only big (as a hand at times), but they even jump! My language helper would laugh when I moved rather quickly at the sight of one, but at least I no longer scream as I used to do in my youth. Then there are the biting flies that leave welts, make you itch like crazy, and, once killed, ooze all your blood they sucked. However, I would rather have those than the huge tsetse flies that sting and gave me an allergic reaction. There are also the other pests that join you in the home: the cockroach, the small lizards, the numerous species of ants, and mosquitoes, to name a few. The "rhinoceros beetles" (aptly named here as the "B 52's") try to come indoors at night as they crash into the screen door or tin roof, After a heavy night of rainfall the termites fly in thousands, aiming for any light. In time we got smart to the idea of putting a lantern in the yard while having no lights on in the house. The next morning the local children would come and collect them all for roasting and eating.

Worse than all these are probably the driver ants (sometimes known as army ants for they march together, usually in lines carrying their eggs, stopping at literally nothing). It is an incredible feat of nature how they climb on top of one another to make a wall and passage for the females to pass through. Although they generally march in these lines, we have seen a huge segment of them covering an area of several square feet, passing over the land as an ominous shadow and devouring any living thing before them. I really don't mind them—so long as they stay outside the house. Occasionally, though, they do decide to make an unwelcome visit. Then you have to either deal with them rapidly, or else clear off for the day, allowing them to go through and clean the house up for you! Once they cleaned out our chicken house and we lost all the chicks, feathers and all.

I suppose the most obvious terror for many people has to be the snakes. We do have many varieties; some are said to be harmless, but I've never given them the benefit of the doubt. I have been both bitten and spat at by poisonous ones, but by God's grace still live to tell the tale; however, in my opinion the only good snake is a dead one. Some of my most frightening experiences have been stepping on a shed snakeskin, because it's so like the real thing. We have the mambas, cobras, the ones with no head and no tail (you cannot tell the difference) and the deadly Gabon viper with the longest fangs in the world. Yes, there are many dangerous animals and extremely nasty "creepy crawlies," bugs of giant proportions and pests that are just an onerous part of living here, but these are all just a part of the African experience.

On the other hand, it is debatable whether you are not more pestered by demanding people at your door morning, noon and until night. All day long they come to frustrate and try your patience before leaving, angry with you for not meeting all their demands. Sometimes they come to sell produce or beg for things and sometimes they merely come to visit. We had to learn what they mean by saying, "I come as your friend," or contra wise, "I come as a stranger," when you know they are not, but it really depended on what need they want met. However, despite all these things prevalent to African culture, God has given me such a love for the country and for the people living here that there has been no other place on earth I would rather be.

Yes, I love the tropical rainforest, hearing the jungle life at night, the crickets and frogs, looking for the fireflies, and listening for the call of certain species of animals out there in the bush (tropical rainforest). We particularly enjoyed hearing the bush chicken and the wea, which is a type of small monkey that makes a call like the siren of an emergency vehicle when leaping through the trees. Then to be awakened by the early morning light with all the birds and their unique manner of talking! Well, I can hardly say "singing" for they aren't at all like those you find in the parks in Britain. You can even guess what the "African Greys" (parrots) might be saying. One type of bird seems to go through an octave backwards down the scale, and others, well, you have to visit Africa yourself to hear those unique sounds, although I am sure you can envisage their beautiful colouring.

Strangely enough, I never imagined there would come a day when I would enjoy living in a jungle, and yet here was the lush growth all around us, more shades of green than you could count and each with their own distinctive foliage. I'll never forget the first pineapple I saw growing, I would stop and look at it every day and just wonder at the manner in which they came out of the ground. I had no idea they grew as a plant, on top of those spiky leaves. Their appearance is red before turning green and then yellow, it is at this point that you must judge when they are ripe for picking, because if they turn completely yellow they will be rotten inside. That's the way it is with so much of the fruit here. The oranges, lemons, and tangerines are all picked while still green, even bananas, which you buy by the stalk. While banana plants may look like branches or even a tree, they too are plants. In fact, the only fruit that made any sense was the green lime from which we make juice as an alternative to drinking warm water, the one thing I really do dislike about living here. I know precisely what God meant in the book of Revelation and his letter to the church of Laodicea when He said they were neither hot nor cold but merely "lukewarm," and He was ready to spit them out of His mouth. I have witnessed Africans doing just that with water that was not cold enough to their liking.

Laodicea was one of the 7 churches to whom God addressed letters (via John) in the book of Revelation

(Chapter 3). It is the one church I remember every time I have disgusting lukewarm water to drink! I'd rather have coffee – even in a hot climate like this!!!

We were coming to the end of the rainy season. There are but two seasons in a whole year basically, dry and wet. I enjoyed both equally for the rain is not like that of England, which tends to be damp, drizzly, and dismal. In the jungle it really rains inches in the space of a few hours, and is such a relief from the hot, searing sun that the children will run and play in it, throwing themselves down in the cool pools that soon appear on the roads. I remember how in 1987 it rained virtually nonstop for six months. We were more than thankful since it was our only source of water for that particular year and we drank from it, washed our clothes in it, used it for bathing— and every other need there is for water. It all came from our rooftop guttering into many barrels. Several nights we were awakened by the sound to run outside and change the barrels all around until all of them were full, wash tubs too! Our children played for hours in the rain (and good old Dad got soaked a time or two). Vegetation thrives here and small plants grow into trees in a matter of months. It's small wonder we call it the tropical rainforest, as there can be no better description.

Liberia held so many positive and happy memories over the five years during which we had previously lived there, and now that we were back again I was excitedly waiting in anticipation for the return of our son Timothy. It had never been easy to have our children go away to school and live in a dorm; in fact, if anything it became harder as they grew older and happier to get back to their friends and social activities there. You are nonetheless a Mum and still feel deeply those pangs of separation. It is not easy to accept that others are training and disciplining your children, doing things you as a mother should be doing for and with them, teaching and training them in the way they should go. Yet this was something we accepted as from the Lord as His best for us at this particular time. We knew that God loved our kids even more than we ever could, and I also knew that my kids had not suffered in the least. Both Amy and Timothy enjoyed our village life during their holidays—and then returning to their friends, and the socialising that goes hand in hand with their education. They would say they had two homes, the best of both worlds, and I am sure they thoroughly and equally made the most of them as well.

Today was the one I would see my son, as I waited I prayed there would be no problems at the checkpoints. Those "rebel boys," as we called them, could be such a pain. Of course they were after money, and that's the last thing we wanted to give them, for we knew it generally went on drink or drugs. They would tell us they were hungry and so we had started to give them some bread and tinned fish, or candy to eat. In fact I recall hearing that once, under the guise of candy, they had been given something for constipation. I cannot remember who in the world would do such a thing, but I'm sure it worked to keep them from the gate for quite some time. On this particular holiday we had invited Arnie Johnson to stay with us; it would be more fun for the lads to have some comradeship. The Johnson family was hoping to become a part of our field, but for now they were our current dorm parents back in the Ivory Coast.

A Place in the Sun October 11-20

Timothy

Our base at Biwiken is basically built around two hills. At the bottom of the first hill, which was the entrance to Biwiken, lay the dorm, along with the basketball court. Johnnie and Peggy Cutts could be found living halfway up the hill, with the Richardson family, Lesley Wolfe, and us living at the top. The workshop and garage were situated in the valley between the two hills, with the second hill occupied by Ken and Rosemary Welch.

For me, it was great to be back. Arnie and I were given the task of cleaning all the graffiti off the walls in the dorm.

It was no mean feat, as the rebels seemed to have glued all sorts of stuff to the wall, making it all the more grimy, frustrating, and not to mention slow-going.

The two-week break went by quite quickly with only the odd taste of excitement. Arnie probably stole the show by nearly stepping on a rather large black cobra that he had not seen while playing Frisbee golf. I have always been a reasonably quick sprinter, but when it comes to snakes there aren't many who can outdistance me in trying to get away.

Added to that were my usual culinary skills. As there were no nearby stores, bread had to be baked at home and I was on one occasion given this task. Much to my misfortune, I discovered that salt and sugar were of a surprisingly similar texture and could be readily mistaken. Quick feet were also needed on that occasion! Arguably, I haven't become much better, but that's a little beside the point....

A Family Vacation

Rosemarie

So it was that we totalled four couples, plus two single ladies and five children, just fifteen of us altogether. The work was hard, making bread from scratch, improvising recipes and keeping everyone fed as we cleaned the housing and cleared the land there. It was a great break to have the kids helping to clean the grounds as well as homes. I well remember Timothy enjoying his father's hobby, that being the art of bonfires. There was much bush to clean out and the fun was setting light to it! Arnie spent days burning out an old stump by our house as he read his book. They maintained excellent attitudes despite the primitive conditions and the laborious tasks that accompany them. Jeni Gillum was a single lady visitor who came over with the children, and I remember my utter astonishment to hear how she made noodles and left them on hangers to dry! We had many fun times together, playing card games and joining together in creative "pot luck" meals. When I needed some peace and quiet, or time to prepare the meal, I'd send the lads and Robert, my husband, off to play a round of Frisbee golf. We had marked out a course covering the whole property that extended down as far as the airfield and hangar, or what was left of it. It generally took them an hour to cover this acreage, but I only had to give it one try to realise that par four or even par five were not within my range.

Our days passed swiftly, as they do in primitive surroundings. They typically included washing clothes and dealing with locals at the door. I was thankful to have Mary come up from the village to do our washing. (It's often been said we have an automatic washer: you put money in her hand, and off she goes to work.) Actually, Mary was a lot of fun and I enjoyed her pleasant company in addition to much appreciation for the toil and sweat that she saved me. Since it was still the rainy season, it would take endless hours and sometimes days to get the washing dry. Out it goes, and in it comes whenever there's a sudden deluge. Because of the nuisance it was to keep running up and down the steps, not to mention the fact that my legs were not getting any younger, I asked Robert to fix a pulley system which would enable the washing lines to be pulled under the roof of the patio. Constructing it was no small feat but, sadly, it never did work properly for lack of the appropriate tools and equipment. We chalked it up to experience and counted our blessings in being able to hear the rain coming through the bush; we generally had about ten minutes' warning before we would get soaked. The lads were very good when it poured, playing games on the bed alongside our new kitten, which seemed to be glad for their company and any attention she might have.

Our days were always interrupted with the villagers coming to sell fruit or vegetables from their "farms." In Western countries farmers plough the land with modern machinery and raise many animals. Africans clear their land with the "slash and burn" method before planting their crops of rice, cassava (manioc), corn, peppers, okra and bitter balls (a variety of eggplant, but very true to its name, I assure you.) Their tools are often homemade, or repaired by the village blacksmith, and of a very archaic nature. A penknife might be a corn husk attached to a piece of metal and this would be used for cutting the rice. Having no guns now, the people had to resort to trapping, and very rarely a hunter would come selling fresh meat, which was quite a treat for us. The only meat I remember specifically at this particular time was the snake; we had tried most things so thought, why not? The meat is very white, but there are bones with every mouthful, since there is vertebrae the whole length of it. At least we tried it, as we had done with many of the animals living in the jungle, from leopard to bush goat or even monkey. The best way to enjoy the "palm butter sauce" (made from palm nuts) is with meat from the bush in it. We also enjoy the chicken, but the size of their country chickens would hardly serve a couple, let alone a foursome including two boys with "hollow legs." The pigeons in Trafalgar Square in London would make a more nourishing meal! We would eat most of their local food, except the termites and the beetles, which they never could convince us were "sweet."

For the most part I enjoyed visiting with people who came up from the village. It was always a real attitude check, especially when you're in the middle of cooking or eating. Every village has its characters and our local one was no exception. Just as you have personality clashes at home, so you do also on the mission field, and while some people were a delight to see, you could tell that others enjoyed the provocation. Actually, we felt really sorry for them, for they too had lost most of their possessions when the rebel boys came down south the first time. Now there were no sheep, goats, cows, or even chickens to be seen. It was said that one man, Tom, had quite gone out of his mind when he lost everything, including a motorbike, which to save up for must have taken a long time. Who could blame them for wanting the most they could get for their little tomatoes or okra they would often bring? We personally disliked

Angels Everwatching

okra, but it was a fresh vegetable and edible if you dipped it in egg and flour before frying. As to the eggs, you had to go to the darkest part of the house and hold them over a torch (flashlight). If you could see through them they were fine, but if not you knew they had been taken from under the chicken. To crack one of those is not a pleasant experience. It's surprising how quickly days pass with just the routine of living.

During the last couple of months Ken and Robert had made a trip back to our old village work and base in Sinoe County. Never will they forget our oldest lady who hugged Robert again and again, calling him by his country name of "Taku." You could say she was more than a little pleased to see the two men again, and they brought back such an encouraging report of their short visit there, along with very sore rear ends from a dozen hours on the back of a motorbike in the pouring rain. Then Ken and Johnnie went to visit some of the country's officials in Monrovia itself, and again were well received by those in positions of authority. We were very encouraged with the prospect of getting back to our former homes and respective village works once again, and I was even counting down the months to the projected goal of getting back to our Tajuoson (*tie-you-sown*) people in Sinoe by April of the following year.

One highlight of that school break must have been our outing to the local town of Pleebo. Although it was just eight miles away, we did not travel to town very often and it was always fun to see what was on sale in their stores, and on the streets or in their market. I loved all the brilliantly coloured cloths they sell in two-yard lengths called *lappas*. That particular time, however, I was able to find some handy containers for flour, sugar, and the like. It was always fun to spend money too. What woman doesn't enjoy that?

The Alarm October 21

As usual, the time passed all too quickly and we made plans for the children to return to school back in the Ivory

Coast, with some others also going to Yamoussoukro for a church-planting seminar. Then we were stunned to hear both from the BBC (British Broadcasting Corporation), and from our own people in Ivory Coast talking on their ham radios (which we could pick up on a normal radio) that everyone should get out of Liberia —and do so at once!

Our field leader, Ken Welch, also received the alarm in Senegal, where he was attending a leadership seminar including matters of contingency, no less. As soon as he arrived, we sat down together to work out the logistics of leaving once again. You could say it was not the happiest of meetings, especially considering that just a couple of short years ago we had lost literally everything. This time, however, we determined that as we went it would be in such a manner as to take our personal possessions. In order to do this we decided to leave a couple of our guys on site at Biwiken, so that our men could continue to watch over the housing and property. Thus it was decided that we would all leave apart from Ken and Robert, but we would do this in stages, taking our most needed supplies out first; and then Johnnie would help bring other possessions across. The programme sounded like a good one and so the next morning we were all set to leave.

The Liberian Checkpoint Charlie
October 22

Timothy

Off we set, jampacked inside the old land rover, loaded inside and out, joggling along the dirt roads until we came to the first checkpoint in our main town, the very same one we had passed just a couple of days earlier. This time there were no civilities, no pleasantries or any teasing; rather, everyone was required to "get out." The rebels stated that they wanted to check everything, but that proved to be just the start of our troubles.

CHAPTER TWO

Harassment

Timothy
 Being a youngster, I was not privy to the politics and events surrounding the warring factions in Liberia. I was able to deduce, however, that things were not as calm as they had been when we had first entered the country. As a consequence, only days before our departure it was announced that everyone would be leaving with us at the end of our break.

Thus it was that I packed, oblivious to the events that were about to unfold. Our journey to the first checkpoint was uneventful and there were groans all round as we were instructed to get out and wait while the general checkpoint palaver took place. We all knew that the rebels were out for what they could get, so it was no surprise to me when one particular rebel took great interest in a digital radio owned by the Richardson family or my Mum's typewriter, which they claimed must be a computer. They asked to see our receipts for everything and they wanted to go through all our baggage. The rebel boys were eyeing Laura so she was told to stand with Lesley, who had her useful dog, Cumin, in tow.

After some time of waiting by the Land Rover, we were told to pile back in, and off we went to the main rebel compound. Knowing that no one had ever had to come here before, I was somewhat concerned, but in all fairness I was pretty clued up as to the Liberian mentality and figured they were just stalling in an attempt to scrounge off of us.

Rosemarie
 "Follow me," said the young rebel on the motorbike. We had begun to feel harassed as the lads at "the gate" had

started to go through our belongings with question after question, but now another "officer" had turned up and told us to follow him. We thought this young fellow was going to see us safely down the road and on our way to the border crossing at the Cavalla River, but we were wrong. In fact, how very wrong we were....

Instead of leading us through the town of Pleebo the young man took us straight to the local rebel-force headquarters, where we all had to unload our cases and go into a small room. Noticeably there were no chairs in this small room, but a small table on which they began to view our personal effects. They addressed Ken as our leader and started to go through his small bag. It was rather hard to account for the cosmetics he was carrying for his wife, and the whole affair would have been funny but for the derogatory way in which they spoke to him. This made some of us rather hot under the collar, so to speak, as we have great respect for our field chairman and to belittle him in front of us was not amusing. I often wonder what goes through the minds of these young men and kids at such times—power over the white man, or just what? They never do believe us that we are equal in God's sight, for it seems they have an understanding that Esau was black and Jacob was white which is why the white man has everything and the black man nothing! At least, that's what our Tajuoson (*tie-you-sown*) villagers used to tell us. The idea of pigmentation is completely unheard of to most Liberians, and, as you may imagine, a very difficult concept to communicate.

There followed some dialogue in which the interrogator told us sharply that the country was at war and had no need of God. This of course, being so contrary to our thoughts, forced us to bite our tongues and allow them to continue their search. This was the first time we had ever encountered such antagonism on their part. After a while of going through one lady's belongings and asking for the use of each article, even they began to realise that this could get very embarrassing. Hence they promptly sent for a lady officer to search the women in another small room while they continued their search of the men.

In the ladies' room—just opposite—we had plenty of explanation to give for the things that could not be understood in their African culture. This rather relieved the tension for a while, resulting in some intriguing and light-hearted comments. However, there was little enough to laugh about as they started to confiscate all letters, papers, magazines, correspondence, cameras, tape recorders, and even washtubs. I was really concerned they might commandeer my Tajuoson language tapes, which were to me as gold, but to them just another incredulous object. They seemed to find some of my letters more amusing than I, who was even more surprised by the fact that one of them could read some English. We really could not understand what they might want with a field paper on Papua New Guinea. I guess they just saw the word Guinea and erroneously perceived potential danger. However, what was most sickening were the papers in which there were articles on Liberia and our work there, along with letters we were carrying relative to this. Each of us began to feel very responsible for the trouble we seemed to be getting into. As if this were not enough, we were accused of lying in their confusion over who had admitted to having a camera and who had not—the problem caused by Jeni and Carol's passport pictures being almost identical. I guess we must all look alike to them, just as they do to us at first. This sick feeling grew as the day wore on....

Timothy

I was with the men, of course, and when my turn came to have my possessions searched I was a little concerned. A few days earlier we had visited the nearest town where I was able to find candy, which was unobtainable in Ivory Coast. In consideration of all those students who had lived in Liberia, I decided to buy a fair amount to take back and share. Due to the lack of packing space available on the Land Rover, we had been instructed to pack everything as tightly as possible. With this in mind I had packed my candy in every crack and crevice available. The discovery of candy in places such as my flashlight and the pockets of my clothes at first caused the rebels quite a shock, but gradually as more and more candy began appearing it became to them an amusing task of finding my secret stashes and causing as much embarrassment to me as possible. In their view, I had acquired the dubious distinction of being called "The Candy Man."

While I hadn't brought much into the country, I had brought my Walkman. When it too was deemed confiscated, for no sensible reason that I could see, I voiced my objection and received in return a torrent of abuse from the interrogator. It was at this point that I began to realise that our predicament was not simply an exercise of the normal "take what we can get" attitude usually displayed by the rebels, but one of a far more serious nature.

Rosemarie

After a thorough search of the ladies we were allowed outside on the porch, where we stood for several long hours. Although we had nothing to do other than think and pray, the time did pass fairly quickly. For myself, I was getting physically sick at the stomach and wondered how all this would develop. I kept going over and over events in my mind, endeavouring to recall exactly what was in the papers taken from me. I knew that one was a letter from Ken and thought that must be the problem. Little did I realise that we all had similar materials and each one of us was going through an unnecessary guilt trip for this intervention. We couldn't think what they could be doing in the building with our men for this length of time, but at least we were outside with air to breathe. The children had been reunited with us and thankfully we had a few things to munch on, and most importantly no one needed the bathroom, or a chair, for there were none. We had little to say, but ten-year-old Mary came out with the best remark of the day when she asked, "Why don't we just go in and tell them what happened to the

Egyptians when they would not let the Israelites go?"

Timothy

The afternoon seemed to drift by in an interminable wait. No one really knew what was going on, as the men had disappeared to be interrogated or something. It was during this time that my imaginations began to get the better of me. Mum has always said that I was born with my sister, Amy's, imagination on top of my own. In times like this when there is literally nothing to do but wait, my imagination can run away with itself, resulting in conclusions about the situation which are hopeful, a little too imaginative for reality, or more often that not, downright frightful. During this time I realised that there was a possibility of our not leaving alive. The more I thought about it, the more I became convinced that this could well be my last day on earth.

Often, especially in movies and drama, immediately prior to an individual's death time slows to a point where they are able to see their own past history in an instant. While this did not happen to me, I was provided with several hours in which I could reflect on the brief life that I had lived and the consequences my death and the death of my parents would have on others. While I could never claim to be expecting to die, the thought more than once crossed my mind that at some point I would be led to a bullet-pocked wall, blindfolded, and promptly shot. Maybe my imagination got the better of me, but the fact that atrocities did indeed occur during the civil war in Liberia helped to substantiate my fear.

Rosemarie

Later in the afternoon we were allowed to walk down to the Catholic Mission in Pleebo, where we could use their facilities and sit down for a few minutes. Needless to say, it was a relief to use our legs and other parts of our body that had been pretty motionless for numerous hours. I would liked to have stayed longer and to enjoy their comfortable chairs, but no such luxury was allowed.

Timothy

After several hours we were herded back onto the Land Rover and taken to a nearby Lebanese house in Pleebo, the storeowners there being good friends of our mission and under these circumstances really kind to take us. There we continued to wait and of course to speculate. Lesley painstakingly took apart a tape she had made to send home and others looked for "any incriminating evidence" they might still have on them. It must also be mentioned that Arnie had suddenly developed a taste for oranges, which was to cause much discomfort a little later. Many among us were feeling nauseous and the cooking of cassava chips in oil did not alleviate this condition.

Night fell and there was still no word of the men, who had been sequestered for interrogation. Then, right out of the blue, one of them burst in and instructed us to jump back on board the Land Rover—we were heading back to Biwiken. The trip was pretty much a blur. All we were interested in was getting out of what felt like a sardine can and breathing some air that had not already circulated through several other people. The ride was made all the more uncomfortable when Arnie's stomach, with only a few miles to go, decided that oranges were not as palatable as previously thought and he proceeded to cover all of us who were squished together in the back with all the orange juice he had downed only hours prior.

Meanwhile, other rebel boys on the road had picked up news of our movements and were waiting to relieve us of some of our luggage on the way home, their favourite pastime it would seem. There was no small palaver when the truck stopped, but since we had "an officer" with us inside the truck we were able to drive on after a few moments, leaving Ken and the other rebel officer, who were on the motorbike, to sort out those lads back there, obviously not pleased at their lack of success on this occasion. Those last few miles were not a pleasant experience.

Our late return to Biwiken brought Dad running. His astonishment as we all tumbled out of the Land Rover was apparent for all to see. Arnie and I headed on home with Mum to clean up and collapse into bed while more interrogations and discussions continued far into the night.

Rosemarie

For me the sick feeling became substantiated while I sat on Jeni's lap —due to lack of space in the Land Rover. Since both Arnie and I were sick, the boys and I were allowed to go home whilst everyone else collected on the Richardsons' porch for a conference with the two officers who had accompanied us back to Biwiken. I was more than glad to fall into bed, even if I could not fall asleep. Meanwhile, over at the Richardsons home both Robert and Johnnie had to make their respective statements, having missed that opportunity in Pleebo. There were demands for money and the two rebel officers finally left with our Land Rover, one motorbike, and their own statement that "We were in no small trouble!"

CHAPTER THREE

British CIA?   October 23

Timothy

As it usually does near the equator, dawn broke the next morning with broad daylight replacing pitch-blackness within minutes. Actions about the house seemed a little more tense compared to the day before, and where previously there were humorous comments and smiles, only silence and worried faces could be found.

During the morning, Barry and Ken disappeared off to Pleebo to what I presumed to be another meeting with the rebels. I'm sure you can imagine the position in which we kids were placed. It was sort of a silent grounding for crimes not committed. Added to this, of course, was the touchiness experienced by everybody simply from the stress that was upon him or her. Being a thirteen-year-old, however, does have its advantages in some situations; I was not put under the same responsibilities or stresses as the adults. In fact, in all honesty (barring the unpleasantness of the day before) it was an extended holiday away from the pain and suffering of my algebra classes. I have heard some pretty wild excuses for missing classes, but I'm sure mine would have won hands down, especially since it was true. It wasn't until the following day, however, that things started to become even more traumatic.

Rosemarie

The rebel officers who accompanied us home took both the Land Rover and motorbike we had used the day before, but they had left us with Barry's motorbike so that Ken and Barry could go back into town the next morning to continue the process of interrogation and investigation. I'm sure the officers would have taken that too if objections had not been raised about having no means of transportation. That Friday turned out to be one really long day as we waited for both of our fellows, and our transport, to come back. We went through our homes searching for anything that might be misconstrued as incriminating and inflammatory and Peggy Cutts even burnt her journal of several years' duration. It was a heartbreaking process and wholly unnecessary, though we did not know that at the time.

One of the problems was the unsubstantiated report of aeroplanes having landing on our airstrip. If you had seen the state of that particular spot of ground you'd have wondered who in the world could possibly begin to believe such tales. Trees and bushes had been growing up again from the lack of attention, there were cement blocks all over the airstrip, and how and where we could have hidden a plane was beyond me. Again it was too ludicrous to be serious. We knew they made up stories about how we pumped gold from our wells at night and at any other time tales so tall would have put us in stitches. Late in the day the two fellows made it back, saying that our truck would follow, but we listened for it long into the night and Robert and I would start at any sound that could be remotely like it. Finally it did come back on Saturday morning, but it was not quite the pretty sight we had expected.

October 24   Intrusion

It is funny how the old adrenaline gets going when you hear sounds. We were in a position to hear a vehicle some two or three miles away and for the longest time you have to wait patiently to see who or what is coming. In this case our hearts were glad to see the Land Rover—until we saw who was in it, and then we froze. It was absolutely full of NPFL rebel boys with their guns, and they had come to look for the two-way radio we had told them did not exist. Of course everything we said was taken as a lie, because almost everything they are told they consider being only a half-truth at best. They systematically went through every home, searching for this radio that we did not have, and at the same time helped themselves to money, jewelry, and such that was small enough to hide away in their pockets.

Timothy

This day, Saturday, was our original day for leaving to go back to school. Instead, we had a bunch of rebels who decided that it was their prerogative to search for any material that might incriminate us as spies. Mum and Dad had burnt everything that even remotely mentioned Liberia in any form, as the rebels seemed to be looking for any excuse to prove their claims. How we, as English, could possibly be members of the CIA I could not quite figure out, but it was a little more understandable considering the fact that the rebels would never have heard of MI5 (the British equivalent in Intelligence) and, according to them we were all one and the same. An example of this was seen a few years earlier when Dad had asked the villagers, in the tribe where they were working, to determine what language the BBC news used. It had been unanimously agreed to be French!

Rosemarie

As ever, there were the funny stories that weren't quite so funny at the time. One soldier boy wanted to look beneath our waterbed to see if we had a radio hidden there! Robert told him that if he had a couple of hours to spare we could empty it for him. Of course he did not believe that it was not hidden there, or that it would take that long to find out. They were also convinced that I had a computer and not a typewriter until I used it for them to see. They were sadly disappointed that I had the receipt for it and other items with me. This was the second time I almost lost that typewriter, the first being in town—not surprisingly, they took a real liking to it.

Our responses to this search were quite different, varying in some cases from a watchful eye to another very different approach of telling them hands off. I remember how Peggy told them they could not help themselves to her knife, and, strangely enough, they put it back again. Those who stayed in their homes still lost some items, as there were too many searching and you could only be in one room at a time. Ken and Rose kept the mission money so we would not have anything but small change in our homes; however they soon found $400 had gone missing from this money. Some of us, however, preferred to keep completely out of the way where we would not be tempted to say anything.

Not unpredictably, the rebels were unable to find the radio we did not have. The whole outcome of this event was their declaration that we were spies and consequently their determination to take all the men up north with them to meet their President. The rest of us were not being held as prisoners, but we were just not free to go anywhere. The four men said this was not possible and "begged" them to allow the two fathers to remain behind, which they allowed after thinking about it. On hearing this I had no peace in my heart. I really sensed that Robert should go too. I cannot explain precisely why I prayed as I did, but I asked the Lord to allow Robert to also accompany Ken and Johnnie if that would be a good and pleasing thing to Him. I knew he would be good as an encourager and felt there would be safety in numbers. My unarticulated request was answered in their very next decision when they again changed their minds, as they were frequently wont to do, and said that only one man could remain. Barry was the most logical choice since he had not only his wife, but all three children there also.

Robert came running to me, asking that I help pack a few things quickly. We had just a few moments to think of what to put into a rucksack. He had been told to take just a small bag, and to fetch it right away. Really, where do you start? There was hardly time to think clearly, but God was gracious, and while I forgot one essential item another wife had remembered to pack it. However, I did remember a Bible and due to lack of space put our tiny pocket one in along with the extra change of clothes and the necessary water.

All too soon the time came for our goodbyes, not knowing if we would ever meet again on this earth. With sinking hearts we watched Ken, Johnnie, and Robert leave, with those few items thrown quickly together, in the old Land Rover full of rebel boys. Others rode away on the two motorbikes, now both of them gone for good. Again we all responded differently, some with tears, some with quiet pondering, but the unspoken question remained, would we ever see our men alive again?

Timothy

As the kids on the base we were herded over to the Richardsons' house where once again we were left to speculate and wait for any titbit of information that might come our way. Eventually, sometime after lunch, Barry came over and announced to everyone present that all the men except himself were leaving to go to the war front and had been given only a short time to pack.

While this was indeed disturbing news to me and to everyone, for some reason I wasn't too perturbed at the time and felt that Dad wasn't going to be long and everything would be resolved once he returned. Whether that was something that I was told at the time or whether it was something that I felt deep down I'm not quite sure, but after an hour or thereabouts, off they went in that rackety old Land Rover.

CHAPTER FOUR   October 24

A full load

Robert

As Ken, Johnnie and I set off with the rebel boys we couldn't have been more surprised when three miles down the road the Land Rover turned right, back towards Pleebo, instead of north as they had told us. We were parked in the town and told to wait there. People came by, asking us what we were doing there and we told them we were being taken to Gbarnga, the war front. One man said he was going to the border so we asked him to tell our people on the other side, who would be anxiously waiting to hear what was happening to us.

An hour or so later the rebels came back and we were on our way, this time heading north, although we soon stopped to take on board a huge basket full of dried fish. Maybe you have never seen dried fish and if you cannot envision what it looks like I am sure you can begin to imagine the smell! In Liberia it is quite normal to cram as many people (or goats, coconuts, bananas…) as possible into a vehicle, so we had four or five other rebel boys with us in addition to the two rebel officers who were responsible for taking us up north. With the dried fish, we were a pretty full and not-to-mention nauseous load.

It was dark by the time we reached River Gbey where we had to go to the lumberyard for fuel. People were told not to talk to us so we sat watching the workers fry some large rhinoceros beetles they were catching in their yard by means of a hurricane lamp. You could say it was not your usual Saturday night entertainment.

As we set off again the Land Rover started spluttering due to water in the fuel, which was fairly typical of life here, so we had to track back to the lumber yard where the rebel boys took us to the home of its Lebanese owner. Thankfully, he gave us something to eat and a coffee—which was to be our last Western-type meal and coffee for a week.

The car being fixed we set off again. The rebels wanted to sleep the night at the next big town, but much to their displeasure we said we wanted to keep moving.

Contingency   October 25

Timothy

As the next day was a Sunday, we had our morning church service up at the Welch residence followed by a contingency plan where everyone —everyone being the adults, of course—discussed possible eventualities and circumstances that might arise. There were practical discussions as well as slightly more wild suggestions, such as making a run for the border through the bush. While it might have been possible to make it undetected to the Cavalla River, there were the logistical problems of crossing it as well as ensuring that the men who had been taken to the war front knew that we had departed voluntarily, as opposed to being taken elsewhere by the rebels.

Rosemarie

I remember well that Sunday as we met together. How do you sing under such circumstances? Paul and Silas were exceptional saints, were they not? However, sing we did and though it was not with great gusto it did lift our spirits to praise our Lord and know that He is our Sovereign Saviour and in control of everything. We read from the Psalms and Barry had a passage prepared for our edification and to encourage us, as it certainly did when we considered God's goodness and how He protects His people, placing His angels around them and watching over them.

What I did not expect were all the suggestions for contingency that we must consider and, as it were, take on board. For one thing, we were to wear trainers (tennis shoes) or walking shoes at all times, ready to run into the bush if necessary. Another item was to pack a "go bag" which should have water, crackers, and small food items in addition to our most valued possessions. We would need a change of clothes and yet keep all this to a manageable size to carry for some miles if necessary. We would number our other bags and cases according to priority. We knew that, barring the unlikely event of being killed, we would be leaving the country and thus if we had room for only one case we needed to know which one was the most important to us.

It seemed that God had given Barry real insight into these areas of thinking, and still another plan he had was in preparation for an unwelcome visit from the rebel boys. If such an event arose, then all the adults would saunter nonchalantly up to the Welches' house on top of the hill, as it was the closest in proximity to the bush. There we would have some games and snacks ready for the kids, to keep them occupied. Meanwhile Barry would "entertain" the rebel boys down below on his patio and in the event of an emergency we could all disappear into the bush. Rosemary Welch would have water on hand and we also devised a "buddy system" whereby each adult would be responsible for one child to alleviate us mothers of being responsible for all of our children. There was exactly one adult per child, apart from Rosemary, who would bring the water, and Barry, who if free would lead the way with a cutlass—a rather necessary item to make a path through the jungle and, of course, a handy weapon for any of the critters that live out there.

Our hearts felt lighter with these practical suggestions and although we took them seriously of course none of us felt it would ever really happen. Once again, how wrong can you be?

After church I went home to start the mammoth job of packing literally everything in the house. Jeni had already packed her few items away so she came to help me out before moving on to assist Carol, who also had plenty to arrange. Since we thought our guys would be freed up north and would go over the border from there into the Ivory Coast, as had happened on a prior occasion, I had to think everything through again and include many of Robert's items in my number one case. Since I also had some pots, pans and my clothes inside, it took the two of us standing on it to shut and lock it up. The laughter returned for a while and it felt good to be busy and making progress.

Heads down   October 26
Robert

Back on the road, the old 1958 Land Rover was making fairly good progress until we came to the Po River checkpoint where our officer in charge, for some inexplicable reason, decided he was not going to go through the civilities of greeting the ones on checkpoint duty. His second in command was driving at the time and so he told him to drive up as far as he possibly could so that the pole going across the road was right up against the windscreen with the bonnet (hood) underneath it! Neither side would give in. Our officers would not get out, and the rebels at the gate would not lift the pole. All of a sudden there were half a dozen men pointing AK-47s at the front of the car. Ken shouted for us all to get down. I was stuck between the two officers in the front and my eyes must have grown as big as saucers to see all these guns pointed right at me! To our incredible surprise the officer in charge of us unexpectedly jumped out and pulled out a handgun we had no idea he had, at which the rebel boys on the gate all disappeared. It was only after a lot more "palaver" that they eventually let us through, thankfully still alive and breathing. This was just one of about 44 gates we had to pass through that day.

With the need of more fuel farther along, our officers asked us for money, but we of course had none. (The fuel at that time was being sold on the road for one hundred Liberian dollars per gallon. Although I do not remember the exchange rate, I do know those prices were exorbitant.)

Since they were not happy at having to pay for the fuel they took more people on board to cover their cost. We ended up with people crammed inside and out, riding on top with yet more guns and, this time, also hand grenades hanging and jiggling from their pockets.

The road was pretty rough; we're talking about something like four hundred miles of driving mostly in second and third gear at best. The jungle was beautiful as we drove past palm nut trees, rubber trees, or bamboo, which is beautiful, but so shady the road doesn't get much chance to dry out. This particular day we were not really taking any of this in. We were just relieved to arrive in Gahnoa, where the people just about fell off and out of the truck, fish and all, but that odour still lingered on.

Rosemarie

I'm not one to treat daily Bible readings like those who read horoscopes, specifically looking for something in it for them that particular day. God does indeed speak to us through His Word, but not often as directly as He did that Monday morning when I tore the calendar sheet off for that day. I put my Wellington boots on right away and dashed up to the ladies, who were now all residing with Rosemary on top of the hill, to share this news with them. How I remember Lesley's dog, Cumin, really getting excited until she saw who was coming. I guess we were all rather jumpy and the sound of those boots, being just like the rebel boys' boots, certainly got everyone's attention. It was worth it though, for just as Barry had drawn our attention to it from the Psalms, the day before, the Bible passage this Monday morning related to God and His angels watching over us so we need not fear what man might do to us. It was God reassuring us yet again. How often those thoughts were uppermost in our minds just then! God has such singular ways of preparing us for what is to come. All feeling mutual encouragement, the ladies suggested having an evening together and eating some of our good food in the knowledge that it could not all go with us. Since our home was the only one with solar lights and the convenience of a gas stove still unpacked, we would hold the dinner there. Then it was back to the packing….

Robert

Having deposited the major part of our load in Gahnoa, we were then taken on to Gbarnga where the rebel boys had high hopes of putting us up in a motel late that afternoon. However the owner wanted money up front, but since no one had any to give they took us to a plain courtyard and gave us one room with one big bed to stay in. Night fell and we endeavoured to sleep two on the bed and one on the floor with a guard on duty outside, but sleep was scarce and you could even feel the rats running across.

Timothy

Sunday and Monday consisted mainly of packing in preparation for a sudden departure. We had been instructed by Barry to pack our baggage in priority so that if we were permitted only a set baggage allowance, we could immediately select the items most wanted. I was more than happy, of course, to dispatch any food that would otherwise have been discarded.

Monday evening Barry came and asked for my help as a lookout. I was intrigued. Off we set to the workshop where a little storeroom was, located at the back. This storeroom was built like any other missionaries' structure except that at the back of the storeroom was a wall of shelves. Much to my astonishment, Barry gently tugged on the shelves and they slid back effortlessly to reveal a cavity capable of fitting approximately five or six tightly packed people. Into this recess Barry stashed all nonessential items that could not be taken with us, such as generators and power tools, and a barrel Mum had packed up, too. When completed, the shelving was rolled millimetres above the floor back into position.

That evening we decided to have a get-together at our house in an attempt to alleviate the doom-and-gloom atmosphere that seemed to cling to every thought and action. If memory serves me correctly, it was hotdogs followed by games. (Trust me to be able to remember the food!) In part, it was also an opportunity to eat some of the "luxuries" that we had at the time, knowing that they would otherwise have to be left behind.

In Liberia, because of economic instability and the lack of more practical facilities such as stores and refrigeration techniques, everyday items commonplace in the Western world were hoarded as if they were gold. I remember one instance when I was able to save enough money ($5) to buy myself a bottle of Coke, which I slowly consumed over a period of weeks. The fact that it was flat for most of that time was inconsequential compared to the mere possession of a cherished item.

We did have a good time, however, and we all went to bed feeling much fuller of stomach and a bit more relaxed. Little did we know that our night had only just begun....

CHAPTER FIVE

Terror in the Night   October 27
(The early hours)

Rosemarie

After our potluck with hot dogs, real ketchup and all those good things that go with them, we were too tired to put the room to rights and so left everything pretty much as it was. Benches that had been brought down were scattered about the room, but the guys could sort it all out in the morning. For now I was rather in a mood to relax a little on the back porch and enjoy the beauty of the night sky.

Living so close to the equator, you just begin to have an insight into the reality of what Scripture says, that the heavens declare the glory of God. We have hardly any inkling as to the vastness of space, and as I looked up the stars were an exceptionally bright spectacle on that particular evening. You may endeavour to count them whilst in the town, but out in the bush, on the darkest of nights they are arrayed in millions above the earth. I've often reflected that's how it must have been on the night Abraham was called to look at the stars. He certainly did not have the disadvantage of street or city lights. At certain times of the year we even have the privilege of looking upwards to the North Star, then turning right around 180 degrees to see the Southern Cross. Some nights you can see the Milky Way and when you think of the words of the Psalmist, "Oh taste, and see that the Lord is good, " you know he was not referring to a chocolate bar. The stars have always held a fascination for me; I've always longed to understand more of their constellations and the significance of their names. Right then I just marvelled at their creation and spent some time singing praises to our Lord.

Thus it was fairly late when I turned in for the night. I was not really sleepy but I knew there was much to accomplish on the morrow. I must have drifted off, but awoke in the early hours in need of the bathroom, and as per usual used a torch to get there and back. I was wearing my earrings and necklace in bed (I do not normally), but after the events of the weekend I did not dare to take them off. It also served as a constant reminder of my husband, who had given them to me. My keys were nearby with a hearing aid, and my shoes were also at the ready by my bed. In Liberia it was essential not to move without a light for the obvious reason that certain creatures might be in your shoes, on the floor or anywhere in the room. Unbeknown to me, others had seen my light and were headed my way.

I was just about ready to get back in bed when I could not have been more startled to hear a voice at the front room window asking me to unlock the door. My first thought was that it was Tom, the crazy guy from the village. We had talked about what to do if he came to the base, and the need to have a whistle on hand, but we didn't have one yet so I could not alert the others by that means. A man's voice spoke again, asking me to *open the door*. I asked who was there, but all I was told in reply was to open the door. It began to cross my mind that it might be the rebel boys, but then I thought, "What a nerve, they would not dare—or would they?" On asking again I was told once again to open the door. Now I was beginning to get a little scared. I called for Timothy and Arnie to wake up because there was a man at the door. I hoped that by doing so this man would know there were others in the house, and of course bearing men's names too. However, once again I was told to unlock the door. I went to the window to speak to the person outside and told him that he must speak to Barry, the man in charge here. He ignored this, telling me again to open the door. This time his voice was rather more demanding so I called out Barry's name as loudly as I could, hoping this would awaken him. Whoever was outside did not take kindly to this and told me to shut up or they would shoot. Now, shooting meant guns and that meant only one thing—there were rebel boys outside the window. Instantaneously I was running across the room into the boys' bedroom and at the same time giving out a piercing scream so as to arouse the whole base to the fact that the rebel boys were here. I told Arnie and Timothy to get down, as there were guns, which they immediately did.

Timothy

Mum coming into my room awakened me in the middle of the night.

"Timothy, Arnie, there's a man outside!"

"What?" I exclaimed, rubbing my eyes and staggering out of bed. By the time I had managed to negotiate my body, somewhat haphazardly it must be admitted, to the door of my bedroom, I heard the ripping of our window screen and the shadow of a body climbing through. Quickly Mum turned and instructed me back inside the bedroom and she followed me in and shut the door. Almost immediately the door burst open with the appearance of a rebel in full combat gear pointing an AK-47 directly at our heads. He told us all to shut up, or he would shoot.

There are some things that have such an impact on us that we will remember them for a lifetime. One of these events in my life has to be my Mum's scream with the appearance of the rebel. I have been to many sporting events and other occasions where screaming is common, but nothing can compare to her sheer ear-piercing scream. We were to find out later, in fact, that it had wakened everyone on the base. If I had not been quite awake before, I certainly was then.

"Nobady move or I kill yu all," the rebel shouted. I don't think any of us could have moved much anyhow, considering the swiftness of everything that happened. It was as if we were rabbits trapped in the headlights of an oncoming car.

"I wan yor monie. Gi me yor monie," the guard said pointing his gun at Mum.

"But we don't have any money," Mum implored.

"You lie, you lie. I wan yor monie!"

"But we don't have any here."

"You lie. I no you gat monie. I wan yor monie," the guard screamed back, this time waving his gun quite threateningly.

I'm not sure what caused me to react as I did. I think it was a combination of trying to stall in order to gain some time as well as fearing the worst for my Mum.

"I gat som monie," I blurted out.

Up to this point the guard hadn't really noticed me as he was more than preoccupied with grilling Mum, but the mention of "monie" quickly grabbed his attention.

"You gat monie?"

"Yea, I get small monie."

"Le me see."

Accordingly I found my wallet and showed him the little money there that I had earned over the previous two weeks. It didn't help his cause too much, however, as it was in Ivorian currency, and it probably was nothing like the amount he was looking for.

"Dis nat monie. I wan all yor monie," he turned away, obviously annoyed with his lack of success so far.

Rosemarie

While this was taking place, across from us Carol had heard my call for Barry. He had slept through that, but certainly heard the scream. Dressing quickly, Carol woke her children and got them organised while Barry came across to our house carrying a huge torch and the traditional baseball bat, though I don't think he quite knew what he was going to do with it. It was not long before he was duly relieved of these acquisitions by the rebel boys on guard outside and ushered into our bedroom, where he flopped down onto a bed from the shock of these events. He was most concerned for our welfare, and we for our part were concerned for him.

Now, George Lott is a very special friend of ours down in the village. When we left in 1990 he watched over our property for as long as he was able to, even at the risk of losing his life. More than once it had been threatened while he remained faithful to us, and more importantly true to his Lord. He was the only believer amongst his people. An amazing thing happened at the very same time we were being harassed by these rebel boys. In his little village home George woke up, (he had no idea why) and felt the sudden urge to get by his bedside and "pray for us people" up at Biwiken.

Meanwhile there were hundreds of thoughts crossing my mind in those passing minutes. Should I unlock the door? Should I put the lights on (which the rebel boys were unaware of) or would that heighten the danger? I was pretty upset with their taking Timothy's hard-earned money, little as it was, and soon realised that they were out for quick grabs. The problem was, of course, that they had guns and we didn't know how many of them there were or whether they had transportation.

As they started telling Timothy to "charge it, charge it" he was putting all his clothing back into his bag that was on the bed, and I started to reason with these rebel boys.

"If you take those, what will the boy wear, what can he put on his feet?"

Of course they were not listening, but it brought back a familiarity with the manner in which we were used to addressing these rebel boys. I saw Ken's tennis racket taken out of Timothy's bag. It had been given to Timothy to take back into Ivory Coast. At the same time I started praying, "O Lord, please don't let them take Ken's racket." It's hard to lose your own things, but to lose those entrusted to your care is another matter.

Timothy

Barry, now disarmed by one of the rebels outside, also faced the growing irritation of the rebel who was not succeeding in what he probably had considered to be an easy conquest. With Mum's reiteration and Barry's confirmation that we didn't have any "monie" the rebels attention turned to a more desperate avenue of both saving face and reaping the rewards of what was probably to them quite a risky operation—he wanted our belongings. In fact, our effects would in all probability fit them pretty well since Liberians are quite petite and we were but teenagers.

As we had already packed in case of a hasty departure, a lot of the things that we considered to be most important to us were already organised in suitcases and bags labelled by their priority. It was not too difficult that night to pack what remained unpacked, as it generally consisted of a few necessities or those things of little value to us. Some of these necessities, however, were *really* a necessity and I wasn't too pleased to be packing literally all my clothes in a backpack. On the other hand, out of respect for and fear of a gun I was more than happy to shove everything into bags in the belief that the sooner I packed, the sooner they would leave.

While there are events that are indeed terrifying at the time of their occurrence, sometimes they can be looked back upon in a more humorous light. There were two instances in the case of the armed robbery that have caused much amusement since, but were not even thought upon at that time. As the basketball court could be converted to a tennis court, I had brought with me some tennis balls. Naturally, when the rebel commanded us to pack everything I did not hesitate to do so. I figured that since the rebels wanted all our stuff they were going to have it regardless of how heavy or useless it might be. It was my thinking that the more difficult it was to carry, the slower they would have to travel and the better their chances of being caught. Upon seeing the tennis balls being placed in the bag the rebel exclaimed, "Wha I wan wid those? I not play basketball." So saying, he threw the balls with the tennis rackets back onto my bed.

The second instance occurred when one of the rebels noticed a bulge in the bed sheets.

"Wha da?" he inquired of me suspiciously. He repeated this several times. We could hardly understand what he meant. He could see the covers, see the pillow, see the sheets, what was he going on about?

Cluing in, I replied, "It de cat."

"De what!" he exclaimed as he grabbed the sheets and whipped them off the bed.

I'm not sure who was more surprised, the rebel boy or the cat, but both seemed to produce clean air between them and the floor. It was the cat that responded first, however, and disappeared before the rebel could move.

However amusing these accounts may be in looking back, at the time they were nothing compared to the fear of having been intruded upon in a place where people find security—their home. Actions were carried out in a daze, in a numbness that cocooned the fear of death. The quick packing of everything into bags and the rebels' constant threats became a blur which could have lasted for minutes or for hours. My aim was solely to get them out of the house as quickly as possible and eventually, after what was probably around ten or fifteen minutes, the last one had climbed back out the window from which they had come.

Rosemarie

We never knew how many rebel boys there were, a couple were in the room with us, but others were obviously busy in the kitchen and my bedroom. Then it went very quiet, a most eerie kind of silence. On all fours I crept into my bedroom, picking up the hearing aid along with the house keys. I was crawling back when I saw one of the rebel boys outside the window. Raising his gun, he shot up into the air. At this point I could not have been more stunned. I was absolutely aghast for I had never really thought for one minute they had real bullets, but evidently they did. On the floor I quickly shuffled back into the boys' bedroom and sat behind the door. Then I shoved my prize possessions behind the bed. My heart was racing, as it seemed they had come back inside and then gone again —and then there was interminable silence.

Timothy

Once the rebels had disappeared, Barry instructed us to stay behind on the floor in my bedroom, where we remained for several minutes while he went to check things out. What had become a blur until now suddenly came back into focus and while we waited crouched on the floor, the shock and horror of what had just taken place began to sink in. I'm not sure whether anyone else realised it, which can hardly be surprising as we were all coming to terms with what had just happened, but I fell into a state of shock. My limbs felt very weak, my whole body trembled like a leaf, and I began to sweat profusely. It took all my thoughts and effort just to control the constant clatter of my teeth.

Barry returned after a short while and informed us that we were all evacuating into the bush. Arnie and I were both in somewhat of a logistical difficulty as all but one of Arnie's shoes had been taken, and all my clothes had been taken. On realisation of this Mum produced my old pair of shoes that had been drying in the oven after they had become excessively wet the day before. This was most remarkable—she had never done this in her life before. Who robbing a house would even think to look there? The other problems were solved once we had dashed over to the Richardson's house, where Arnie was provided with one other shoe from a reject pile and I was supplied with a pair of jeans from Laura's wardrobe. Although obviously wide awake at the time, it took me several seconds to work out just how to button a girl's pair of jeans while holding onto a flashlight, which was the only source of light permitted.

Rosemarie

All holding hands, as we had done in crossing to the Richardsons', we now made our way up the hill to the four ladies at the Welch's home. (Rose, Peggy, Lesley and Jeni were sleeping in the one house since the men had been taken.) They were naturally so anxious to know that we were unharmed. For my part, I was glad to see them up, dressed, and ready to go. Hearing my scream had achieved the desired effect and in fact they were on their way down the hill when the rebel boy fired his gun into the air, obviously to scare them back off again. (It certainly succeeded as they had all turned tail and run back.) Without more ado, not knowing how many rebels there might be or when they might come back again, we put our contingency plan right into action. In the middle of the night and holding hands with our "buddy," we followed Barry out into the bush.

CHAPTER SIX

Exodus   October 27, about 2:30 AM

Timothy

Once we had all gathered, we trudged single file into the bush. I'm not sure how long we walked but I would guess it wasn't more than a mile or so. There was no talking on the way; the only sounds were the crunch of feet on leaves and the rustle of clothes against plants.

Our destination appeared to be no different from the terrain that we had come through, but it was here that we sat out the night. Sleep was nonexistent and yet again I was placed in a situation where I had a lot of time on my hands. This time, however, my thinking was a little more productive.

In all honesty, my life so far had been a comfortable one. While I knew I was a Christian, I had no special desire to search after God and serve His purposes. My aim in life was to succeed, have plenty of money, and live life to the full. I simply had no need for God in whatever circumstance arose; I felt more than capable of resolving it to a satisfactory conclusion. I felt in control of my own destiny and, barring an odd hiccup, things were all under control.

The last few days, however, had completely reversed my thinking to the point where I realised that I had no control over my circumstances and was therefore forced to rely on someone who did. It was probably at this point in time that I decided to let Christ into my life – not as Saviour, because He already was – but as an active *participant*. It's sad that it took my being twice at the point of being fearful of my life before I began to ask for help. Sitting there in pitch-blackness with various insects and critters scampering all over me, I asked God to help me.

It would be nice to be able to say that all of a sudden a wave of relief and comfort came over me and that I felt warmth and encouragement never felt before, but this was not the case. The chorus of a popular Christian song did pop into my head, however, and it never ceased to help me during the following days: "He's got His angels watching over me, every step I take. Angels watching over me."

No real surprises occurred during the night. Everyone was uncomfortable with all the insects that seemed to be able to find their way everywhere and there was a fair amount of scratching going on. The crickets were incessant in their chirping, and once or twice a bush chicken squawked away, surprised at our presence in their territory, but there was not much movement save for some of us tripping over a root or while trying to find a little privacy to relieve himself.

One particular sight (which captured my attention for much of the night) was the part of one plant that had a fluorescent surface. It was either that or a moss growing over the plant. While I never did discover what it actually was, I could not figure out how a bark that hadn't seen light since 6:00 p.m. the previous evening could remain fluorescent throughout the night. I was reminded at this key point in my Christian life how important *detail* is to God.

Rosemarie

Our time in the bush was none too comfortable, especially for me; not dressed quite as the others and it felt really damp. Actually, I was so thankful to the Lord that I was wearing a jogging outfit as pyjamas, (which was pretty unusual.) The fact that my husband was gone and I had been on a waterbed had prompted this idea for extra warmth. You know, God takes care of everything, even the smallest details of modesty. Again, I was amazed when I thought back to the fact that my shoes had been right by my bedside! They had been a careless oversight of the rebel boys. Since I have particularly small feet my shoes would probably have been a better fit than those of the lads, but God had blinded their eyes to the shoes even when they were where they would almost have tripped over them. Then here we were, far removed from any others who might return to our base that night, and I certainly had much for which to be thankful.

As the minutes and hours ticked by we all had our thoughts and times with the Lord, who we knew was present with us. I thought how appropriate had been the verse of that morning, so why indeed had I feared these lads with their guns? Then I prayed that the theft had begun and ended with our house and that they would not touch any of the others at all. I also thanked God for leaving the tennis rackets; then my thoughts turned toward the language tapes that had been right at the top of my "go bag." I knew they had taken this bag, it was already packed to carry, but with eyes grown accustomed to the dark I had seen the flask of drinking water left behind, but could not recall what else. Thus my mind started turning to all the things I knew I had lost for sure: pictures of the children, especially done for my fortieth birthday (our daughter Amy being so far away from us back in England) and a clock that was a particular gift from Robert's brother. How would we ever tell him it was stolen, but "O Lord," my heart cried, "If those language tapes are gone then I can never return to that work and pick up the pieces again." Having especially been prepared for our furlough, they were the only thing left from our five-year work amongst the Tajuoson people in Sinoe County, where we had lost everything two years ago, including our culture file, dictionary, tapes—the lot....

I wondered if anyone could possibly sleep here, and later found out that many of us had comfort and consolations from the Psalms and other such passages of scripture. As for me, I was reliving events and began to think of the cat and some of the funny sides of the whole incident. In fact, being really tempted to laugh, I had to suppress it for if I broke out laughing I knew they would all think I had really lost it!

We were all rather taken with the luminous leaves in the bush, so ordinary by daytime, but such beauty shining out in the blackness. As I think back on it now, it reminds me of some lilies that bloom only at night. The only one who sees them is God, but like all creation they are there to magnify and glorify Him, our great Creator. There are many things we miss in life, but He sees them *all,* and right now He knew where we were and saw us in His infinite love and tender care.

As I wondered how many more hours could be left, not having a clue of the time, I was aware that a bush chicken was getting closer and closer to us. I was having extreme difficulty in staying put as it got so close that it almost stumbled on us and took off with no small clamour and screeching. At this I was able to release the suppressed laughter and found I was not the only one. It was such a relief to stand up and be able to talk once again.

Barry reviewed the situation whereby we wondered if we might need to continue hiding or if we might even walk from here to the border. He cautioned us to be quiet and said he would go back to our base and check it out. If nobody was there he would go to the village and find George. Hearing the village bell, we felt sure that they must all know of our eventful night and would soon be coming to look for us. Barry said that in case of the rebels' return he would pull out a couple of larger things from our secret room which would placate them. He asked if we were in need of anything. Peggy was suffering from wearing flip-flops in the bush and I really needed some underwear, but wouldn't you know it, Carol had some with her and they actually fit. That's more than a store can often do when they are brand new. It may be noted that Carol has an exceptional gift in the area of helps, and any practical needs may often be met through her in the most extraordinary places or circumstances.

It was hard to wait on Barry, but finally he found us again, bringing George with him. Barry apparently had been totally disoriented in the dark and we were far removed from the position he had thought to lead us. George, for his part, was absolutely astounded to see us there and to

Angels Everwatching

hear of our adventures. The village people of Tugbaken, a mile away, were quite unaware of any visitation from the rebel force, although they had heard the gunshot, which they took to be a hunter. Some of them had heard boots walking through the village, but wisely they had stayed put in their homes.

George led us out of the bush again, and as we came up the hill some of the villagers came the mile up to Biwiken to tell us how sorry they were. Some of them were even crying. When I saw the broken screen at our home again, it was my turn to cry. The reality of what happened hit me like a slap in the face. However, I had to get busy, as Barry had given us only an hour to have a shower and move back up to the Welches' home again. I was thankful my wash lady had turned up and there were both water and people on hand to help. None of them could believe we had spent a night in the bush. Over and over again they would ask us why we would risk our lives out in the jungle where there are snakes. I simply told them that I would rather be in the bush with God than out here with the rebels and their guns. The snakes and other dangers had never occurred to me in the least—again another small sign of His gracious protection and goodness.

Safety in Numbers — October 27

Timothy

Upon our arrival back at the base, which incidentally was much quicker than our exit, since this time we were able to see where we were going, I headed back to our house to see what was left of our possessions. As I came up the hill there were suitcases, clothes and other items strewn all over the grass. We also found the hat of one of the rebels, which later turned out to be of significance. As I have mentioned previously, we had packed according to priority and Mum had packed some suitcases so heavily that they could not be carried. In fact, one suitcase—her number one priority, no less, was so heavy that it had been left inside, the rebels being unable to lift it out of the window.

Once things had been picked up and placed back inside the house I took a look around outside. Apart from the torn window, it was as if nothing unusual had ever happened. While the physical appearance of everything remained unchanged, more obvious was the trauma each individual had experienced, with the telltale signs of nervousness in both actions and speech.

Another council of war, so to speak, was quickly organised and the wood stove was lit to make the coffee. This was such a small action, but it fried the one radio we had left, which we had used to listen to the BBC and our folk talking over in the Ivory Coast. The others and I were totally unaware Barry had hidden it in the stove when he came back to check out the base, and he had forgotten about this prized possession, but again we learnt that we can live relying on the Lord and upon Him alone. It was determined that from now on we would stay together in order to discourage a repeat of the night's events and the Welch home was determined to be the most practical, I think because of its size and proximity to the bush.

Rosemarie

Having made the decision to stay at the Welch home, Lesley and I spent an hour or two on the swinging bench outside on the back porch, where we welcomed people from the village who came up to visit us while Rosemary and the other ladies arranged rooms and a meal inside. We felt utterly exhausted, without energy to do anything at all. After a sleep that afternoon this changed, as I became a bundle of nervous energy for the next few days, getting things packed away, overseeing the lads as they worked helping others, fetching wood and water, but also ensuring they had some play times too. Sometimes I would help with meal preparation and other times busily do whatever job there was to be done. The world would say that we were bound together by our circumstances, but I prefer to believe it was the Lord. Some of us packed, others cooked, and they did a great job for we really ate well, and working together was actually fun. For my part, I saw the Lord pulling us closer together, giving us a love, unity and appreciation for each other as only He can.

Timothy

The rest of the day was taken up by transferring everything from all other houses to the Welch residence. Ironically, we lads did not have much to move compared to the others as nearly all of it had all been removed for us by the rebels.

During the afternoon another group of rebels appeared having heard about our break-in. Upon their departure, they left behind one rebel who was instructed to guard us in order to discourage further attempts to break into our homes. He set up camp down near the Richardsons' and how he expected to guard us from 150 yards away I don't know, but to tell the truth I would rather he had not been there at all. None of us being too happy with this situation, Barry also employed some of the local men from the village to keep watch with him, which cost us not just in monetary terms but in food, fire and other comforts they asked to keep them warm throughout the night.

This discomfort was somewhat alleviated when Barry announced that George would also be staying in the house with us during the night, without the guards' or villagers' knowledge. Being so concerned for our safety, George left as if he were going home, but made a detour through the bush and came up at the back of us and in through the back door, and slept on the floor of Ken's tiny office. Barry also informed us that he would check in on each of us during the night.

I think everyone was a little concerned about going to bed that night, myself included. I did feel a lot safer with others around me, however. Throughout the night Barry came in to check on us, and each time his flashlight woke me up just in time for me to tell him that we were okay. I'm not sure how many times he came in during the night, several I think, but the next day he asked Mum whether I actually sleep. I think that if even one of the many frogs outside had been croaking out of sync with the others it would have awakened me that night.

CHAPTER SEVEN

October 28-29

Robert

Some hundreds of miles north in Gbarnga, our main concern was the water situation, as we had brought only a small amount of well water with us. As a result our guard accompanied us into town, where we found a Lebanese store. We told the owner there that we had no money, but he "just happened" to know Sam in Pleebo, our local town, thus we were able to get what we needed on credit and pay later via Sam. Thus in God's goodness we had bottled water to drink, crackers and some tinned meat to stave off those hunger pains. It was left to the local village people to feed us. They were very good, but you can only take so much peppered "palm butter" or "greens and rice" for breakfast, dinner and tea! (Or in the US: breakfast, lunch and supper.)

Rosemarie

The same morning down at our base in Biwiken we were still pretty worn out, none of us having slept too well, which was hardly surprising considering the circumstances. I cannot even count how many trips I made to the bathroom and back during the night. It was like undertaking an obstacle course in my endeavour not to disturb Lesley or her dog, sleeping at the foot of the double bed that Jeni and I shared. I would relax until memories flooded the mind, and then I'd be wide-awake again.

It was almost a relief to see daylight and be busy again. Since I was up so early (some unearthly hour like five o'clock) I got on with the day's washing. The rains had set in again and thus we were often running in and out, changing the washing around on the lines to get it all dry. I remember wearing a nice dress passed on to me by another lady, and, when it was admired, voicing my wish that Robert could see it too.

Barry called us all together after breakfast and we worked out a programme according to what needed to be done in each house and who was free to do the cooking. This plan worked well and was repeated after dinner. Peggy, Carol, and I still had quite a few edible and household items to pack away, not to mention solar lights and waterbeds that Barry would pack up for us. We needed to be ready to take everything with us if possible, as a soon return no longer seemed likely. Two years ago the rebels had used our base for their headquarters and after a very nasty experience of having left the bathrooms intact we decided we would also remove all sinks and toilets. Hence there was still a lot of work ahead.

As to the younger task force, they were allotted the job of fetching and hauling wood for the stove and water for our other basic requirements. We certainly were thankful that the wells still worked after the last couple of years and rebel occupation.

Packing literally everything was a long and arduous task, which was not made easier by the odd villager who came to see what we might part with as a leaving gift for him or her. It was almost like the vultures hovering over their prey, and it was particularly hard to maintain a consistent walk with the Lord and a cheerful manner in these circumstances. It was very definitely a period of testing as we got our things up to the workshop, where we stored them, and determined what clothing, kitchen or food supplies we might possibly take out with us, and what to give away. Then how do you decide which has priority—personal property, or the kitchen stove? These were hard decisions we each had to face, but I remember that the stove finally rose to number four on my list.

As night fell we could tell Barry was feeling the stress of responsibility for all of us ladies and all the children too. When I walked outside, I was warned to be careful of the water and found he had laid traps at strategic points. Inside, he placed coke bottles on each window ledge, and he also placed umbrellas upside down close to the screens. No rebel could enter this house unannounced! Rather amused at this and some of the funnier incidents, Lesley, Jeni and I started recalling them in our room. The result was quite uproarious; in fact, we were making so much noise that Rosemary came in to ask whatever the amusement could be about. It just felt so good to let our hair down and laugh at the image of us all back there in the bush: Arnie with odd shoes, Timothy in Laura's jeans, me with my bright red jogging suit, the playing of baseball with tennis rackets, the scared cat and the many incidents that were really rather ridiculous, to say the least. It lifted the tension no end before we all turned in for the night.

Again it was not easy to sleep; I was unconsciously listening for any noise or sound that might resemble a rebel car or activity. Repeatedly the Lord brought to mind that His angels were there, and I knew Barry had the same confidence. I'm sure that's the reason any of us got any sleep whatsoever.

Robert

Most of our time during those few days up north was spent outside under a tree, talking with the local village people, who were extremely kind and courteous in every way. Generally we would talk with them about a host of different things. Most of them wanted to get out and go to live in America. We felt sorry for them in many ways, as they were trapped; they were not permitted to go anywhere or to do anything.

Our guard was with us for the main part, but we could hardly go anywhere. The two rebel boys who had brought us so far from our Biwiken base were joy riding in our Land Rover. They came to see us a couple of times, but they didn't tell us anything. However, it was a good time just to sit, reflect and pray. Ken had given his Bible away, but Rosemarie had put the tiny one in for me so that was all we had between us.

While we sat and watched the evening star come up I realised that Rosemarie would be able to see that too and I wondered how she was getting along and what she would be doing, how the packing up was going. I thought about Timothy and his activities and in what way he might be involved. Then there was our daughter and other family members' back home. I hoped and prayed they would not be too worried.

We felt pretty secure, really. The only time there was any real threat of death was back at that one checkpoint—apart from those loonies who hung grenades on their belts as they joggled up and down on top of our truck, maybe.

One miracle was not getting sick from a lack of coffee, which was a surprise.

I wondered about the possibility of walking out if we were not given our vehicle back and how far it was. The days seemed neverending.

One night we were sitting outside talking when we saw a satellite go across the sky. We jumped up watching it and the people wanted to know what we had seen. How do you begin to explain a satellite to a native of the bush in West Africa?

Timothy

Down at base, another night without the unexpected brought a few more smiling faces to the table, although understandably everyone was still pretty tired and tense. Yet we were still all well and healthy and the packing up was almost complete. Things were beginning to look brighter again.

Rosemarie

This Thursday did indeed turn out to be a defining moment in our situation. We had our usual meeting to decide who should do what. Most of the packing up was now completed and I was asked to tackle the tools in the workshop, getting them stored into barrels there. Barry, meanwhile, thought it prudent to send for help as we were under such duress. It was difficult to continue with our night watchmen who were taking advantage of our situation, and us living all together like this. The UN had been out to see us after hearing that the rebels had taken our men up north. They promised to do all they could from their headquarters in Harper (also known as Cape Palmas on the coast), but we hadn't heard from them in days. We had talked about the logistics of sending George to the border, but we didn't want to do anything that might jeopardise his life, and he was well known for his close relationship with us. Finally we all agreed he could go a few miles south to the town of Pleebo to the Catholic Mission and ask if they had any ideas that might help us out.

You come to a point where the verse in 1 Corinthians 10:13 is so true. The trial seems to be too great, but God never does give us more than we can bear. I think that point had now been realised and was materialised that afternoon in our reaction to hearing the approach of a vehicle. Had George already arrived in Pleebo and was this help coming, could it be the UN, or was it more rebel boys again? We breathed a sign of relief when a white man with two ladies who were said to be nurses drove up, having received our message for help at the Catholic Mission.

As we all met together with them we listened to their suggestions, which we then discussed while they took a walk around our grounds, leaving us to think them through. Basically they laid it on the line suggesting that we were living under too much pressure, which was not good either for the children or ourselves. They came up with a proposal that we should send the children to their Mission in Pleebo along with a couple of the ladies to care for them. Should we be stopped they would say the children were in need of their nurses' attention. They told us that these ladies were just that and our children were sick—if not physically as yet, they were in such a harrowing position that relief was necessary for them at this point. As we thought and talked about it we saw the wisdom in this. It was indeed no lie that our children were in a nerve-racking situation and we all liked the idea of having them under the safety and roof of these people who were familiar with the war situation. The Catholic Missionaries had lived through it these last two years, but were not yet harassed by the rebel boys as we had been. Thus we agreed that the five children would leave with Jeni who was our visitor and Carol as a Mum. We felt that the three of us whose husbands had been taken should stay, remembering that although we were not prisoners we were just not free to go anywhere. We did not want in any way to endanger our men who had been taken captive. We talked over the possibility of Timothy being a go-between. The Catholic people were willing to visit us daily with him and verify that we were safe while at the same time they would be able to bring any needed supplies and take baggage out as they went. Timothy was none too thrilled with this idea in the least!

As soon as our new friends heard our agreement things happened with lightning speed. They told us to pack as much into their little truck as possible. They suggested, for example, that our kids would need mattresses and bedding, food supplies and clothing, and all those sorts of things that were legitimate for us to send out with them. I undid some of the suitcases and packed yet again, this time bearing in mind that Timothy had very little in the way of clothing. Thus I packed his Dad's clothing in his bag and reorganised everything for a third time.

In no time at all the van was packed full to capacity and soon after Jeni, Carol and the children (Laura, Brian, Mary, Arnie and Timothy) were on their way with our prayers that they would be allowed through the checkpoint. The instant they had gone Lesley took her dog for a long favourite walk, and we all let her go, knowing that she needed to get away for a while. Others started to rearrange the furniture and rooms, now that there would be seven fewer in the house. For myself, I shut the bedroom door and really let the tears come that had been welling up inside for a considerable time. My husband was gone up north, and who knew whether he would be released or killed? Our sixteen-year-old daughter Amy was back home in England, probably worried sick, wondering what in the world had happened to us. My son was off to the town and comparative safety;

and here I was, still in the bush. This was no pity party but a realisation that all four of us were truly separated, and I had come close to the point of more than I could bear.

After just about an hour we heard another vehicle and we could hardly believe it. Our hearts began to sink when we saw that the Catholic van was coming back. Our first thoughts were that they had been turned round at the checkpoint. As they came closer, however, we saw just a man and lady there, no children and no luggage. Best of all, they were cheerful and really smiling. Apparently in Pleebo, where the Catholic Mission is located, they had happened to see one of the military officials from Harper who had been absent for a while. On hearing of our predicament and night theft he was horrified and said we should all come into town immediately. This was great news. Again we hurried to pack the van with as many things as possible, deciding there would be time for one more run that evening.

Thus it was that Lesley, her dog Cumin, and I went first, leaving Peggy to help Rosemary get her household things together and come later with Barry. We were informed that we should be allowed to collect our baggage the next day because it could all be stored at the Catholic Mission in an old chapel there. This news was almost too good to be true. When we got to the checkpoint we were held up, but not for too long. Cumin took rather a dislike to the rebel boys there, and it would seem those feelings were mutually reciprocated.

Arriving at the Mission, I noticed Lesley's earring was missing, but thankfully we found it in the truck. It must have dislodged with all the kafuffle at the checkpoint when her dog would have liked a rebel boy for her supper. A small item, but very valuable, and those small things were the many blessings for which we thanked our Lord.

Timothy

The Catholic Mission, having heard about our plight, had come out to offer us refuge at their quarters in Pleebo. I'm not sure of the in's and out's of the deal, but mid-afternoon found us packing once again into the Catholic Mission's vehicles heading back to Pleebo. This short trip, of course, meant that we had to pass that now infamous checkpoint. This time, unexpectedly, there were no problems.

I had been to the Catholic Mission several years earlier when the basketball team had gone there for a game. My responsibility at that time had been as water boy.

Once we had unloaded, we were shown to our rooms which were positioned in a dormitory form, where each room was connected to one long hallway. While we were still technically under house arrest, and therefore banned from outdoor exploration or any travelling whatsoever, the blanket of suppression that had been more than evident at Biwiken felt a little lighter. Sometimes it's better to be a kid.

Rosemarie

One would think that we should all have slept well that night as we were all totally exhausted, but it seemed the neighbourhood dogs thought we still needed guarding. Thus we all tossed and turned, with their barking all night long, and still of course at the back of your mind is that unanswered question: "Where do you go from here?"

Robert

Up north on that Thursday night we were ready to go to bed when our "two guys" pulled up with the Land Rover and moved us on to Kakata. We didn't really want to go there because it was not far from the battlefront. Having no choice, we set off, it being too dangerous to travel during the day. Amazingly, they stopped about halfway and offered us a cold pop. That was an unexpected treat in the middle of nowhere.

About midnight we arrived at their headquarters, where they showed us a little room. This time there was no bed, just a cement floor with only a rice sack for a pillow! As you can imagine we didn't get much sleep that night either.

CHAPTER EIGHT

Patience is a Virtue   October 30

Timothy

Another night had passed safely. Another day dawned and "us kids" struggled to relieve the interminable boredom of being "grounded." Thankfully, however, someone had had the foresight to include a pack of Skip-bo cards in their luggage and it was upon this game that I spent the day's energy.

At this point, in an endeavour to explain my eagerness to join in the fun, I feel it's worth mentioning my history with card games. I have always been a sore loser when it comes to anything competitive, to the point that I would often have to be disciplined as a child. Much to my parent's grief, however, I've always had a natural affinity for card games and I think that as far as Mum and Dad were concerned, I did not lose often enough to learn the merits of losing gracefully.

While Skip-bo is predominantly a game of chance where card counting and the like are of little use, I had more than my fair share of wins and thus the hours passed quickly. The little grey cells were further enhanced when someone appeared with a tub of black liquorice, which took two days for all of us to consume.

Release

Robert

When Ken, Johnnie, and I got up the next morning a new Colonel—or maybe he was a General—said we would be seeing the Vice President that day. As we sat waiting people would come asking questions why we were in the country and why we were not working up north. We told them other missions were working with village groups up north, but our base was down in the south of the country and we worked in different locations: namely with the Grebo (Maryland County), Glaro (Grand Gedeh County) and Tajuoson (Sinoe County) ethnic groups.

About dinnertime the General said, "We need to eat." Since we had no money he graciously took us out to lunch at a restaurant next door; it was the inevitable greens and rice.

Shortly after we had finished our meal a brand-new Nissan Patrol pulled up. The driver spoke to the General, who told us to gather up our belongings and get into the car which had been sent to take us to the Vice-President.

Off we shot pretty quickly. As we approached the checkpoints the driver flashed his lights, up barriers went, and we drove straight through without even slowing down. This seemed unreal to us after our checkpoint experiences during the long and arduous journey up north. Suddenly we turned down a small dirt road leading to a school and pulled up outside one of the buildings. We were told to get out and go inside, where there were some chairs and a table with all our papers spread out upon it. There were our passports, letters, papers, magazine clippings, and all the correspondence that had been confiscated from us!

A couple of men were sitting behind the table, one being the Vice-President himself, whom Ken had already met earlier in the year. His first words to us were, "This has all been a big mistake!" Can you even begin to imagine our feelings and thoughts upon hearing those words?

The Vice President then proceeded to explain how they needed us in the country and the work we did, adding that in our paperwork there was nothing derogatory towards their organisation. He apologised profusely for those responsible for this ordeal. Having done nothing wrong we should never have been brought north. Any news we had even referred to in our papers was nothing new or different from that broadcast by the BBC.

Another man then came into the room wearing jeans and a tee shirt and carrying a rocket launcher over his shoulder. As he took a seat close to the Vice-President I wondered who on earth he could possibly be? He was later introduced to us as the Minister of Internal Affairs! The General joined our party and they each echoed and emphasised the words of the Vice-President: they wanted us in the country, they were extremely sorry for the whole affair, and then the Vice-President asked if there was anything he could do for us.

We had decided before we went to see those in authority that it was best to let each one talk in turn. Whoever was asked questions would reply without interruption from the others. In this way there would be order of speech without confusion. We found this worked extremely well, and it was so true that when you stand before kings or those in authority God will give you the words you need to say at the time.

Ken now spoke up and the first thing he asked for was an official letter granting permission to travel back down country and to take all our belongings out of the country. The Vice-President turned to a secretary who was present at this meeting and asked him to go right away and type this up so he could sign it there and then. The Vice-President then asked if there was anything else. Ken replied that we had four hundred Liberian dollars stolen from our base while the men were searching it. Upon hearing this, the Vice-President told the General to ensure we would be reimbursed before leaving. We lastly noted that the journey was long, money was short, and that petrol was being sold at premium prices, so he said we might have twelve gallons from his house back in Gbarnga.

Soon afterwards the secretary returned with the paperwork we required and the Vice-President duly signed it for us. The meeting ended cordially. We all stood up and shook hands as we said our cultural goodbyes, the General offering to accompany us to find our truck. As we walked outside Ken looked at me and said, "Well, what do you think of that, then?" I could say positively nothing for the tears that were welling up in my eyes. It had been such a surprise, not only our good reception, but their whole demeanour and manner of treating us too.

Thus we all piled in the General's car and went back to the main road turning towards Gbarnga. We had gone only about a mile down the road when along came our Land Rover, going at some ridiculous speed for its age. It was probably travelling about 60 mph to my thinking, with our two illustrious guards at the wheel. The General flashed his lights and the truck came to a stop, but we could just envisage the driver pumping away at the brakes in his endeavour to stop it when travelling at that kind of speed.

The General came up alongside the Land Rover and all he said to the two officers was two words: "My office!" We followed them to Kakata and on the outskirts of the town the General stopped at a house, went in and came out, giving Ken the four hundred dollars they had promised. We then continued into the centre of the town to the General's office and pulled up alongside the Land Rover. The two rebel officers were standing beside it. We asked them for the keys, but they were not inclined to give them to us. When the General told them to hand them over, they reluctantly did so. They then went inside the General's office, and as we say, I'd like to have been a fly on that wall!

While they were gone we checked over the Land Rover, putting the necessary oil and water in it. We found there was no oil in the back axle so we took care of that problem too. After a while the guards came out and, leaving the General behind, we returned to Gbarnga—this time we were in the driving seat with all our paperwork, passports, and correspondence back. We also informed the guards that we would not be taking passengers, and certainly not dried fish.

About halfway to Gbarnga the truck started overheating. We stopped for a look and saw that the water pump was leaking. We managed to find some water in a stream and fill it up again, but by this time it was getting dark and, discussing the situation, we decided it would be sensible to stop at the Phebi hospital, which was run by the Lutherans and situated on the outskirts of the town. By the time we arrived there it must have been eight or nine o'clock. We parked the truck inside the grounds and while Ken went to find someone in charge, Johnnie went to look for fuel and I was left guarding the vehicle. As I was putting more water in the radiator a nurse passed by and asked me what the problem was. I explained to her that the water pump was leaking. On hearing this she told me to follow her. Locking the car, I followed her into the hospital—and guess what the first thing I smelled was? No less than hot, fresh coffee. Did that ever smell good!

We had planned to drive back home through the night, but the doctor took one look at us and insisted that we were not going anywhere. He said that we needed a decent night's sleep and we could stay there overnight, sleeping in one of their houses. We asked the doctor about fuel, as we would not have enough to get us all the way home even with the Vice President's contribution. He recommended another group on the compound who might sell us some. Johnnie and I went round to see them with the four hundred dollars that had been given back to us, the only money we had. We asked the people there if they would be willing to sell some fuel and they asked how much would we want. I told Johnnie that it might be sensible first to ask their selling price, since on the street it was one hundred Liberian dollars for just one gallon. At that rate we had only enough to purchase four gallons! We were told that he would sell it for the same price he paid for it; and this turned out to be twelve dollars and fifty cents so we were able to buy about fifteen gallons.

After a most welcome cup of coffee one of the nurses took us to a house with three bedrooms; we gave one to the guards and used the other two for ourselves. Thus we each had a bed, shower and a good night's sleep. The doctor said that we could see the mechanic who works for the hospital in the morning.

Rosemarie

Back down south in Pleebo we were enjoying the delights of fresh bread brought in from the town. The kids loved it so much they needed nothing on it. They would come into the dining room and just pick up a baton of bread to eat (similar to a French baguette). It was a wonderful gift.

Barry was well occupied going to and from our Biwiken base with the one Catholic fellow who was able to give his day to our pursuits. The few miles to Pleebo did not take long since the dirt road had been recently leveled. We helped unload the truck each time. By the day's end most of our furniture and belongings were safely stored away with us there. Everyone seemed to be taking a greater interest in our plight, from the UN to local storeowners. There were even rumours circulating around that the rebel boys who had broken into our home had been caught and that the stolen belongings had been retrieved.

One evening Barry got together with us ladies in the little chapel to discuss what message we might send out worldwide via the BBC, having been encouraged that this would be a good thing to do. We spent some time putting together a statement that would not be taken as derogatory to the rebel cause and yet at the same time asking for the release of our men and ourselves too. The message to be sent across the border would also include our nationalities, to point out that we were not all Americans and thus could not possibly be CIA spies as it had been claimed.

A Long Day   October 31

Timothy

The following day, which happened to be a Saturday, was a continuation of the previous. Even I was becoming disillusioned with yet another card game.

Sometime in the afternoon, I was informed that everything that had been stolen from us had been found and brought to the Catholic Mission. I was taken to a room where all of our things had been thrown on the floor, quite literally, and I was told to go through it and determine what was still missing. I did so although it was actually quite hard to remember what I had brought over with me, but there were without question items still missing—including my brand-new shoes.

One of the lessons that I learnt from the robbery was how little we actually need. Although most of my things that were returned were indeed useful, I had become accustomed to living without them and while I was happy to see my things again I had learnt that possessions were not my be-all and end-all.

Robert

Upon rising the next morning in the hospital we went to find the mechanic. One of the rebel boys had gone into the town, while the other stayed with us. The mechanic had a look at the truck and agreed with us that the water pump was beyond repair. We could not imagine where in the world we were going to find another water pump for a 1958 Land Rover in the middle of a war-torn country.

As if the mechanic could read our thoughts, he said that there was a fellow locally who had three old Land Rovers sitting in his yard. We went to see if he was willing to sell us a water pump. We discovered that yes, we could purchase a water pump, but for the princely sum of four hundred dollars, for which he would be willing also to fit it. Having bought the fuel we did not have that much money. He just said sorry, if we could not pay that price there was no water pump for sale. We begged him, after the manner of Liberians, but he still would not come down at all in his price. Upon hearing all of this, the hospital mechanic told us to wait a minute and he would come back. So saying, he disappeared.

He returned about a quarter of an hour later, telling the man to fit the water pumps; the doctor would pay the bill. They actually ended up fitting all *three* water pumps because the first two were no good. This took most of the day, and it was late afternoon before we were finished. The doctor had meanwhile given us and our guard a good lunch. The last water pump was now fitted but still leaked a little. Our mechanic disappeared again and this time came back with a little tin. Opening the top of the radiator, he took some powder from the tin and put it in the top of the radiator, telling us that by the time we had gone a couple of miles down the road it would be sealed up. We asked him what ever could be in this tin. He duly informed us that it was snuff!

When the repairs were complete we took our leave of the doctor, arranging to send the water-pump money we owed him to his wife, who was in America. We then set off to find the UN headquarters in Gbarnga and had gone only a few hundred yards when remarkably a UN truck came by. We flagged him down to ask where their HQ was located; and it turned out to be back along the way we had come, so we followed him there. Here we solicited their help to transmit a radio message down south to their Cape Palmas HQ, asking them to let our folk know that we were officially released and on our way back down south to them. They were quite willing to do that for us.

Having taken care of these formalities, we drove into Gbarnga to pick up the other guard. We then drove to the Vice-President's house and waited on the road while Ken, one of our guards and some house security guards went up the drive to pick up the promised fuel. While we were waiting a guard of the Vice-President's house said that I was taking pictures of him. I could not comprehend how he could think so, but he repeated his statement and glancing at my watch said I was using it to take pictures of him! As it happened, my watch being broken, I was wearing Timothy's. His was one of those fancy ones with segment changes every 10 seconds so it was continually moving. Maybe I could have understood the guard's wild imagination if he had seen science-fiction or detective films, but where he got this idea I could not conceive. So I told him that I would put my hands behind my back, which I subsequently did.

Then this same guard proceeded to tell me that "You Americans" are all the same. I replied, "You can't paint us all with the same brush." He asked what I meant by that. I told him you have some good Americans and some bad Americans, you have some good Liberians, and some bad Liberians, some good English and some bad English, and then he understood the point. Of course by our skin colour their assumption is that we must all be American and subsequently all the same.

By this time they had come back with the fuel, but only nine gallons and not the twelve as the Vice President had said. Putting it in the back of the truck, we were asked to "carry" one person with us, a soldier. After some discussion we agreed and it turned out to be a blessing down the road.

Rosemarie

Desiring to spend out time profitably at the Catholic Mission, we again made a division of labour so that we were all usefully occupied. I took over the laundry, which I did in the shower room, and spent many hours running in and out with the incessant downfall. We finally had to string it all on indoor lines around all our rooms. The girls didn't like this too much as we had decided on a room inspection to keep them enthused and tidy. They later claimed this was why the boys had won on the room check with Peggy as our impartial judge. I myself could hardly believe it and had to go and take a peek at the boys' room. I was astounded by their cleanliness and organisation—even their dirty washing was folded up! Carol and Peggy took over the organisation of all our baggage, making an inventory in case we had to leave anything behind, and again arranging everything by priority. I must say they made a wonderful job of what had looked an utter mess in the old chapel we were using for storage.

We managed to get nearly everything back from our base at Biwiken apart from what was locked away in our secret hole. Sadly, those things had to stay there, where they were subsequently found by a local village scoundrel and hence lost to us forever.

I couldn't have been more flabbergasted when they asked me to come and view our stolen possessions that had been found. The culprit had been caught, apparently identified by the hat he had left behind. There were my cherished photos, the clock, and many other items that I instantly recognised, including, would you believe, my typewriter. Amazingly the third attempt to take it, but yet still there! However—we did lose many things, from clothing to bed covers and umbrellas. Although some of those items were real needs, this time they seemed minor in comparison to all we had lost from our home out in Sinoe back in 1990. I'm sure it will not surprise you to hear that our Lord has more than replaced these through the ensuing years.

Saturday evening we were in for a real treat. The men at the Catholic Mission said they would play a video for us. That may sound quite ordinary to you, but video systems in Liberia, and during the time of war at that, were rare in the extreme. Sadly, the ones we chose did not work and the one we watched was absolutely ridiculous. Again we found that the things of this world do not hold the worth or charm with all the answers we sometimes think they do. Rather, we have far greater treasures living with Eternity's values in view. However, it did pass another long evening of playing the "waiting game."

Timothy

How can one forget the room inspection that took place during our stay at the Catholic Mission? Can a boy be cleaner than a girl? Surely that's against the "rules," but alas, we were to be rule-breakers and even with the disadvantage of a female judge there could be no doubt that our organisation and efficiency surpassed those of the opposite gender.

In all fairness, the truth of the matter was that we were subjected to room inspections on a daily basis at the dorm in Yamoussoukro, and as Arnie and I lived in the same room there we were accustomed to cleaning and tidying quickly. In fact, we also won the cleanest room for the semester, if memory recalls. This was no advantage to the present situation, however, as the girls had also lived in the dorm and were subjected to the same army-style inspections. So as far as I'm concerned, credit must be given where credit is due.

Reunion   November 1

Robert

Setting off for home, we arrived in Gahnoa, making pretty good time, and from there proceeded until we got to the same checkpoint where we had had the life-threatening problems earlier. In the end we left them to their palaver and fell asleep in the Land Rover. We must have been there a couple of hours or more when abruptly the dispute seemed to be over and off we went again. That's the way life is in Liberia, one minute there seems to be no solution and then all of a sudden, most unexpectedly, everyone is happy and the problem is solved. This is very typical of the African palaver;one minute you feel sure someone will soon be hurt, and then, surprisingly, everyone is shaking hands and content with their resolution.

As we were driving down the road we saw reflectors of a car that appeared to be stuck in the mud. We stopped and the occupants asked us if we could tow them to the next town. We needed to put the truck into four-wheel drive and agreed to tow it as far as the next town, but not any further due to the shortage of the fuel situation. Of course at the next town they wanted us to tow them still further, but we felt we could not. As it was, most of our driving was once again in second and third gears at best.

As we came up to the checkpoints, the soldier we had taken as a passenger would lean out of the window and give the rebel boys a few shells for their guns. Thus we had no further problems going through any of the other checkpoints.

By morning we came close to Zwedru and saw a very small child of about four years just standing in the middle of the road. Naturally we stopped and got out of the car to determine the problem, but as soon as we all did the rebel boys called us to get back inside quickly, for it was a trap. The small boy was being used as a ruse for an ambush whereupon we might have all been shot. This again is not unique to a war situation. Travelling in West Africa, you dare not stop when people wave you down for help, or even buy fruit at the roadside, for out from behind those bushes will appear men with their guns, after your vehicle or whatever they may be able to take from you. You really need God's wisdom in taking passengers, or stopping to help the proverbial damsel in distress.

Rosemarie

Another Sunday—and so much had passed in the short time of one week. We had shared some things and prayed together from time to time, but this day we would again worship and praise our Lord. I've found that when I'm hurting it often alleviates the pain to just sing and take the focus from myself to my Lord. This morning I was having a most enjoyable time going through the songbook when we had an unexpected visitor.

Timothy

Sometime on that morning, shortly before our Sunday service, the UN representative reappeared with news that Dad and the others had been released and were on their way home. Apparently a contact had seen the Land Rover passing through Zwedru. This caused much excitement and inevitably even more speculation as to when the men would arrive. There was further concern when someone mentioned that they might get the wrong impression to find no one there when they turned up at Biwiken.

Rosemarie

You can imagine the change in us all upon hearing this news. As we rejoiced together our hearts were so thrilled with the goodness of our Lord. It was not an easy situation for us, in that the Catholic men joined our little service after

Angels Everwatching

just receiving the news that five of their nuns in Monrovia had been murdered, some of them they knew personally, white ladies too. However, they "rejoiced with those who rejoice" and listened to our testimonies of how the Lord had helped and encouraged each one individually during our trial, especially of the Psalms and the many passages He had brought to mind out there in the bush.

As we shared new things we were also learning from this experience. One of their men taught us a new and most applicable song:

He's sweet, I know, He's sweet, I know,
Storm clouds may gather and strong winds may blow—
But I'll trust my Lord, wherever I go,
For He is my Saviour, and He's sweet, I know.

The afternoon was the hardest part of the whole time for me, simply waiting for my husband to arrive. Some of it I spent repacking yet again and sorting out the clothes I knew he would need on arrival. We also did a reshuffle of rooms to accommodate the guys. This being done, I just wandered aimlessly around both inside and outside the grounds, praying for their journey in anticipation of their arrival. I was longing to show him the sign on one of our rooms, which read, "God only made so many beautiful heads, the rest He clothed with hair!" That had to be a classic. I tried to picture them arriving at our base, wondering what in the world they would think, but surely the local people would tell them. This must have been one of those "longest days in your life" experiences.

Robert
Arriving in Kahnwiken (*cow-we-can*), one of the larger towns, we managed to find something to eat and pushed on towards River Gbey, where again we had to stop at the lumberyard to deliver some letters. From there we headed for our Mission base at Biwiken. As we drove nearer the local people were coming out on the side of the road,

shouting and waving to us, seeming really happy to see us back again. This was one of the reasons we wanted to drive ourselves—to show people that we were in control again.

We turned off the main road up towards Biwiken and parked on top of the hill, but were shocked to find no one there. I looked at our house and saw that one screen was ripped, but everything had been cleared away, so we went back and headed for Pleebo. As we were going towards our old base and village at Tugbaken (*two-bar-can*) we saw George, who told us that everyone was at the Catholic Mission. We hadn't a clue as to what had happened, and all we were told was that our people had spent a night in the bush.

I think that was the fastest ride to Pleebo we had ever made.

Timothy

In the end, as dusk was quickly setting in, the men were met by a multitude of emotions. There were people both crying and laughing, some silent, others trying to swap stories as fast as they could talk. Dad looked not much different than when he had left several days ago except he was rather thinner, and in dire need of a shower and shave. He came up and gave me a hug with his usual "Hullo little fella!"

While there were a myriad of emotions going on all at once, I felt detached from the scene, no sudden elation that Dad had arrived back safely. Maybe it was because I did not realise the danger he had been in, but I always believed that he would return, so when he did appear I was not surprised or overcome, simply because I had already anticipated it.

The only other reason I might not have felt any emotion may have been due to my own male pride. Growing up, I always viewed emotion as a weakness. I had been raised in a dorm where I was the youngest boy and therefore had to face a fair amount of torment from the older boys. When I cried or had a "pity party" I was mocked for being a "cry-baby" and I had learnt to suppress my feelings and hide how I really felt. Even when I was in shock after the robbery I was constantly biting on my lips to suppress a natural reaction, which would have displayed my weakness. My emotions were without doubt far more reserved than most.

Rosemarie

I cannot even begin to tell you how I felt to see Robert safely returned from the war zone. Immediately it hit me how much weight he had lost in just one short week or so. I have never quite witnessed such an event where quite literally everyone was so ecstatic to see everyone else; the hugging went on for some time with the genuine relief that obviously flowed through us all. Robert knew nothing other than that our base was completely cleaned out; upon hearing that we still had a lot of missing property he called to one of his guards who came over and noted the main items that I could recall. I was struck by the familiarity with which Robert called this man and reasoned that some changes must have been taking place in this respect.

The guys of course were beat and ready for a good shower and a hot meal. Some stayed up late telling their stories whilst others of us just crashed, being content to hear their tale early the next day.

Robert

Pulling into the Catholic Mission, everyone came out to greet us. I received the biggest hug by my son and wife, asking them if everything was alright. Rosemarie said, yes, and asked if we had heard what happened to them. We had heard they spent a night in the bush—but we were yet to learn the whole story later.

After something to eat we had a meeting and decided we would leave the country the following day.

CHAPTER NINE

Freedom　　　　November 2

Timothy

The next morning, some of the men left in order to locate a truck big enough to take all our goods across the border. I, of course, was left behind and once again we had to go through the process of packing up.

After finding an Ivorian truck in town, that "just happened" to be going back empty that day to the Ivory Coast, the men had to decide whether to go back to Biwiken for the remaining things we had left behind or to go into Harper and pursue their missing motorbikes. In the end Barry and Ken did go to Harper, but although they caught sight of one of "their lemons" (as we had nicknamed them) they never did get to retrieve the motorbikes.

Rosemarie

Once we had packed all our belongings ready for our final move there was not a lot to do except to wait, but we were so pleasantly surprised by the arrival of visitors. Some of the storeowners we knew had come by; and then Rosemary's wash lady, along with her sister who worked for me, came to tell us goodbye. This was so very special, as it is particularly discourteous in their culture to go without the appropriate leave-takings, so we were very touched.

One final visitor was George who came with Peter, another village friend from Tugbaken. Not knowing if he would make it in time, George had sent a letter ahead, and, as Rosemary read this out to us, we were so touched that we cried.

Robert

We were getting ready to have lunch when Timothy and

I went into town to purchase some cold pop for everyone. This would indeed be a real treat, but we could sense that the atmosphere towards us had changed. There was some hostility, leaving an impression that we were not as well accepted there as before.

Timothy

The men arrived late in the afternoon with the Ivorian truck scheduled to leave that evening. Because the border closed at 6.00 pm we had to rush, throwing everything into the truck as quickly as possible. One incident especially stands out at this time. As I was carrying something particularly heavy to the truck and passing by one of the Catholic missionaries, he said, "Oh, you'll get good marks for that." I can assure you that getting "good marks" was the last thing on my mind just then.

We all piled in, with Mum and one of the guards in the Catholic truck, the other women in the Land Rover, which Ken drove, and the rest of us guys in the big truck. Because we were in a bit of a rush, the driver had no intention of a pace that would respect either the road conditions or truck. I was in the back with all the baggage and it took all my energy to keep from being squashed. I did not complain at the time, however. I wanted to get over the border just as much as everyone else did.

We arrived with mere minutes to spare but were hit with yet another setback. While up at the war front, Dad and the other men had been given a paper that granted us permission to pass through all checkpoints and to cross the border. This time, however, the rebels decided that our documentation was a ruse and that we had faked it! How they decided the signature was a forgery when they had never had a real one to compare it with is beyond me, but that is the nature of Liberians.

Eventually, however, one of the guards that had travelled to the war front with the men testified to the authenticity of the document, and we hopped aboard the barge. As we crossed the Cavalla River, it would have been nice to be able to say I looked back and experienced an overwhelming number of emotions. The truth is that the only thoughts that crossed through my mind were the ones that I had experienced earlier when we had returned from England. While Liberia was ravaged by war and continual upheaval, there before me remained the beautiful green expanse of jungle, unaffected by the struggle. The one lasting memory as I looked back up the single-track road was that it could well be the last time I ever stood on what I had always considered to be my home soil.

Rosemarie

Our truck was the first to arrive at the border. The "first in command" guard was sandwiched between the Catholic man and myself and this had provided a good opportunity to sing and talk of our Lord, but his face was cold, hard, and, I supposed, a reflection of his heart at that time. Our paperwork went through smoothly—much too smoothly, I thought, and continued to look out for the big truck to arrive. It was not long before we were on the barge and cranking the wheel to pull us across the river. Although I strained to see it, the truck conveying my men was still nowhere in sight, but then land was receding as we crossed the short distance to the other side.

I'm sure all of us ladies had mixed emotions at that point. For some it would be relief, and in fact I do not think you begin to realise the stress and tension you are really under until you are taken out from it. Some were even laughing, but for others it would be sadness about the whole situation. Then again there were thoughts of our return. Would it ever materialise now after all these events? For myself, I wondered if I would ever cross those waters again. Would I ever get back into Liberia, to Sinoe County and our Tajuoson work there? I felt sick at my stomach, asking, "How long, Lord, before we may return?"

There were no tears; the pain went deeper than that, right down to the depths of our hearts for the situation, and more especially for the people we were leaving.

Robert

Our big truck was the last in line to leave; we had some Liberians on the back with us in addition to Arnie, Johnnie, Timothy, and me. We all had different thoughts: from the potential dangers of checkpoints, the practicality of standing with the baggage—holding on wherever possible down dirt roads, to Johnnie—wondering what in the world was a guy from Texas doing in a place like this. It certainly would seem bizarre, one day shaking hands with the Vice-President and just a couple of short days later leaving the country in the back of a truck!

When we got to the border road my thoughts were, how in the world would we ever get down there in time, knowing how long it usually takes? Yet it was as though the Lord picked that truck up and just moved it down the road in a ridiculously short amount of time. We have never travelled that particular road so quickly, ever!

Our arrival at the border was the provocation for a big palaver with the rebel boys there because of all the goods we were taking out of the country. Our two rebel guards were still with us. The argument centred over the paperwork signed by the Vice-President that the rebel boys at the border claimed was a forgery. The guard in charge of us then said he had been there when it was signed (which he had not, of course, since they had been joy-riding around in our Land Rover at that particular time.) However, this statement was accepted and the truck driver was told to get the truck onto the barge quickly as it was time for closing. He nearly tipped it over as he drove from land to water and onto the barge.

We all followed the truck onto the barge and were ready to go when David, the guard second in command who had been with us all the time, called, "Robert, come back, I need to talk to you." *Oh no*, I thought, *whatever now*? I jumped off the barge wondering what the problem could be, until he said, "Robert, make sure you come back, we need people like you here." I told him that yes, Lord willing, we would be back again.

I wondered what it was that this one guard has seen to make him say this. He saw that we did not have to threaten anyone the way they did. We did not have to point a gun at anyone to get what we needed. He had seen how the doctor had provided for our needs and we had been able to provide our guards with beds, whereas they had given us a cement floor to sleep on. They saw us live before them without quarrelling as they constantly do, and with just a completely different way of life from theirs. This is nothing but the grace of God and we had seen His hand at work all the way through.

Rosemarie

Over on the Ivorian side of the river we found a couple of our own missionary guys, Gary and Bob, who had sat the day through as usual in the hope that one day we would make it to the border. (We later learnt that Gary and Bob had spent every day scouting the border roads or just sitting at the border, waiting for us to show up.) We had been looking for someone there, but missed them at first as they must have been talking or walking. They had the biggest surprise when we came off the barge. It took the Ivorian authorities longer to get through all the "red tape," but again, it was not long enough for me as there was no way I was prepared to leave the border until I knew that our men in the big truck were safe.

Then, after what seemed hours, but I guess was really only minutes, there was the big truck at the border, on the Liberian side. After some time it was driven onto the barge, but we were horrified to see how the truck toppled right over. It swayed badly, but then righted itself and how that thing never ended up "in the drink" I'll never know. God must have literally placed it back upright again. I felt for sure the fridge had fallen, with many other things tipped over inside, and hoped none of our menfolk were in there with it! I found out later that, incredibly, nothing had moved and everything was still intact—yet another miracle in the making.

All week long we had been saying a new expression we had learnt, an Americanism that "The fat lady has not sung yet." The barge made quite a terrible sound as it was cranked up and turned to move across the river. We all said that now the fat lady was finally singing—and it was music to our ears.

Robert

When we got to the other side the customs officers there wanted to charge us customs on everything that we were bringing into the Ivory Coast. With most of it having been brought into that country in the first place, this was a bit hard to swallow. Gary and Bob gave them a hard time since they had been coming to the border every single day for the last ten days, looking for us, and the border authorities knew the situation anyway, so in the end they simply let us go.

We now had three vehicles—a large red Ford truck, the Land Rover, and the big truck with our belongings. Gary had brought his motorbike so I volunteered to go with him. Despite being the last to leave we were first to make it back to the town of Tabou and went directly to the house where Sonya, Bob's wife, was so relieved to see me. We told her that the rest of our folk were on their way, but we were going down into town to phone our mission in Yamoussoukro. I personally spoke to Frank, the field chairman, who was more than relieved to hear that we were all well and safely out from Liberia. By the time we got back to the house everyone was there. We emptied the truck out onto the porch and hired a guard for the night.

I've already said that Bob and Gary were two of our missionary guys. I do not know how to briefly explain more about them… Bob was part of our Liberian field team and Gary the Ivorian field team. Together they watched out for us every day at the border.

Rosemarie

Bob had that day driven our big red mission vehicle to the border and a few of us had the luxury of travelling in comfort that last hour or so back to the home Bob and Sonya were renting in Tabou. Sonya came running out with obvious relief and joy at seeing us alive and well. How she fed all of us so quickly was a remarkable feat, but we were soon ready for the night, which for me was disturbed only by dreams and the shedding of those tears at memories of what we had passed through.

I was particularly worried what Arnie's Mum, Sue, might think or say and many needless fears filled my mind. Although Sue was the dorm mother for the Liberian field MKs I had only recently met her, and yet we had placed her son Arnie in a very dangerous position. Rosemary, who was sleeping with me, quickly reassured me that everything would be fine. I was just plain worn out.

Timothy

We arrived at the Ivorian town of Tabou later in the evening. There was quite a lot of confusion at first because no one knew who would be coming or when and it was not easy to find sleeping room for so many people. Despite close quarters we managed, and the following day we kids set off for Yamoussoukro so we could get back to school, of which we had now missed more than a week.

Rosemarie

Down in Tabou there was one small problem, namely, that of getting everyone transported back to our Ivorian mission base. Gary had been travelling the roads for days on his motorbike, but he instantly offered to go all the way up and then back the same day to bring us extra transportation.

The next morning it was decided the children would travel up there that day. So it was that Barry, Carol and Jeni travelled up with them, giving the rest of us an extra day to relax at the ocean and come to terms with the adjustments of being back in the Ivory Coast. Only a river separated Liberia from the Ivory Coast and yet the two countries might as well be hundreds of miles apart, for their differences.

Lesley, Robert, and I had a leisurely stroll down to the sea where we sat for a long time on the rocks, watching the waves, the fishermen bringing in their catch, and wondering what our future might be. There is something very therapeutic about the coast and watching the tides come and go; I could have stayed there for days. However, the next morning, after hearing the results of the American presidential election, we set off for the very long drive back to Yamoussoukro where our folk were waiting to receive and welcome us back.

Species   November 3

Timothy

Our return to Yamoussoukro created quite a sensation within the school. Suddenly, I was the focus of much attention. We arrived just as the school day was ending and many of the students and teachers came up to the dorm to glean information. I cannot say whether I enjoyed the sudden attention or was embarrassed by it. It felt as if I were a newly discovered species that everyone wanted to examine and observe. Life returned quickly to normal as I was immediately back into my place both at the dorm and school. Mum and Dad arrived to even more fanfare the next day and were placed in somebody's home while meetings took place to discuss the future of Liberia as a mission field. Somewhat selfishly, I was personally hoping that the work of our mission in Liberia would be closed simply because I now wanted to live with my parents. When Dad came by one evening a few days later and informed me of the official closing of Liberia I was secretly pleased—I knew that either we would go to another country or Mum and Dad would remain in Yamoussoukro.

It was hard adjusting straight back into school and the dorm after a couple of weeks as intense as those we had just lived through, and normally our mission requires you to return to your home country for some time of debriefing after such an experience. However, in our situation, and since we were so many, they brought a very gentle counsellor with our mission over to see all of us there in the Ivory Coast, having sessions twice with each single and each couple, and once as a group. Mum and Dad also suggested he should see me, which he did on one occasion. Apparently he found that I too had undergone much trauma, having realised the danger more than the younger kids. That was their blessing, but on deliberation mine were the greater learning experiences, and also a turning point in my Christian life.

Robert

When we arrived back in Yamousoukro, after a few days of rest we all had a meeting together and were told that it had been decided to close the field of Liberia until further notice. At the time this was one of the hardest things to hear because we knew where our Tajuoson people were going when they died. We figured that the best language learners were only about halfway through to any kind of fluency in their tonal, nasal and incredibly difficult language, thus none of them had yet heard the true gospel of Christ. Having been back to see them not too long ago made this doubly hard.

Rosemarie

What Robert calls a few days of rest was to me more like a week of sleep. We would sleep all night and then some days after breakfast go right back to bed again. Sometimes we stayed up until the afternoon, but I don't think there was as much as a whole day where the two of us were able to stay on our feet. We were both utterly exhausted.

During this time, however, was the special blessing of having Trevor McIlwain with us, the author of the *Firm Foundations* chronological teaching books who was leading a seminar series on church planting. It was such a joy to sit under his ministry and observe his obvious love for the Lord.

Our mission crisis-management team came directly to Yamoussoukro, from Senegal, and we had to relive each moment for them, but it was good to meet with our counsellor and just talk through those things that hurt. It was amazing to me that at our second chat when he asked how I felt now, I could just say, "Father, forgive them, for they know not what they do." In one short week with rest and relaxation you really could look back again objectively and see how lost those poor rebel boys were. We had a group discussion also in which our counsellor really encouraged us not to give pat answers to people undergoing stress. I will never forget that wise counsel and have found a hug or just being company to someone really does go a whole lot further than giving out scripture we all know and would apply. He had a cute picture to show us of a zebra losing its stripes and saying, "I think I'm going through stress!" That was a good one for our prayer letter.

Above all I was crushed by the decision to close our field. It was not a surprise, but that did not take away the sting of that finality. For five years we had worked at learning the language of a people who are totally lost and bound for hell. Was it all for nothing? I've had to come to terms with the loss of a son, the loss of a foster son, and other losses in our lives—but nothing came even close to the loss of our work and witness among the people in Liberia. I had to learn the lesson of thanksgiving all over again. Job became a very precious book to me in the ensuing days and even in the years since.

That night after we were told our field was to be closed I wondered how in the world I could ever go to bed and sleep. Amazingly God sent the biggest storm, the door banged shut, the waterbed rocked, and I just felt myself drift off into the best dreamless sleep. I will never forget the experience of that night when our Lord just simply took His poor hurting child up into His tender loving arms and held me.

Robert

As you look back you see where the Lord puts you in a position where you cannot do anything else but trust and rest in Him. I think that is where you get your peace in some situations. Also in scripture it says, "I will give you the words to say when you stand before kings and those in authority," and He certainly put the right words into our mouths at the time needed. It all comes back to the fact that we do "walk by faith and not by sight." (1 Corinthians 5:7)

* The letter George wrote was subsequently printed in our Mission magazine, *Brown Gold* 1993.

Epilogue

Timothy

This is probably the most difficult passage to write in that it is a time of reflection and realising just how much things were out of our own control. I can see how many ways God guided and protected us. Through the last several years I have continually remembered and taken comfort that through both trials and tribulations of all kinds I have had "His angels watching over me." Our experiences in Liberia completely changed my perspective on life. I learnt that, in myself, no matter what abilities I possess or how well I think I can control a situation, I can do nothing without the help of Christ. To my shame, it took two "life-threatening" experiences for me to realise and accept this. I sincerely pray that you will not need the same encouragement.

Rosemarie

Years ago (1985, in fact, and just a couple of weeks prior to flying to Africa for the very first time) we encountered one of those "angelic incidents" that at the time you do not recognise for what it is. We were up at the north end of Scotland in a borrowed car, on a country road in the middle of nowhere, and for some unknown reason the car just stopped dead. Robert did not have a clue as to what could be wrong and went off to a house to use a telephone. While we were waiting the kids and I prayed about our situation. Robert had barely reached us again when a brand-new car pulled up behind us and the driver asked if he could help. The man not only knew where the garage was which could offer assistance for our particular make of car, but also offered to tow us there. Wouldn't you know it, the *only* thing he had in his boot (trunk) "just happened" to be a towrope! In no time at all we were on our way and soon arrived at the garage.

To this day none of us can remember what the man looked like or how he disappeared with his car, for when we turned to thank him he had literally vanished. The problem was so simple it was fixed in an instant—we simply needed to change a control on the car from summer to winter (we were up north now). Later on our way home, the thought came to me that this was no ordinary incident, simply from the fact that there was no explanation as to where the man came from or where he went. Why did he have only a towrope in his car, and a brand-new one at that? I recalled the verse from Exodus which we had recently read together in our devotions: how God sent His angel to prepare a place for them. This had really encouraged our hearts in relation to our preparations for going to Liberia and now it had been reinforced beyond doubt that He truly was preparing His place for us too.

Our most recent experiences in Liberia were quite different—there were no angelic appearances and no towropes, yet God was everpresent, meeting every need along the way. Really, how in the world can you expect to fix a 1958 Land Rover in the middle of a war-torn country? How can you begin to find fuel enough to get back home, and at an affordable price? When I think of His marvellous protection for us in the jungle that night, even the smallest detail of it, without rain during a month of heavy rainfall was just incredible. It's those kinds of things that send shivers down my spine.

While writing this little book I was reading a passage that really fits our experiences over those few days: "…the things which are impossible for us present no difficulty to Him. It is only as we are brought to the end of ourselves that we learn to really look outside of ourselves and turn unto Him who never fails those who fully trust Him."

We were exactly in this position, as Timothy found out; there was absolutely nothing we could do to help ourselves.

God delights in manifesting His glory in impossible situations. We saw Him intervene again and again on our behalf. He undertook for our physical needs, giving extra measures of strength to keep going in the face of adversity—we did not realise how much until back in Yamoussoukro where we not only slept long hours at night, but mornings and afternoons as well. He undertook for our mental needs, keeping our hearts and minds stayed on Him, and, as ever faithful and true to His Word, He undertook for us spiritually, bringing us through the trial to the praise of His glorious grace and of the many lessons we learnt in and from it.

Those were the kinds of days never to be repeated and I'm sure they will not be, at least, not in the same way, for the Lord delights in working in so many and *various* ways in our lives, and I've yet to see the same things happening twice. Though it was an experience none of us found the least pleasant to go through, it was one of which we could all say we were glad to have been there and had a small "taste of the Lord's goodness," as it were. We had the awesome privilege of seeing Him provide as no other could; of His sustaining us in the direst of circumstances; of His giving words to say at the right time and guarding our tongue at others; and the fulfilment of His promises of abundant grace to meet our every need. We proved Him beyond any expectations as Saviour and Lord of our lives—of His love, tenderness, care, longsuffering grace and mercy in abundance. We cannot praise Him enough for allowing us the privilege of passing through a fiery trial to declare His glory among the heathen and to share it with you also. It is truly one of those times you would never choose to relive, and yet we are so thankful we were all there together, united in seeing God at work on our behalf and in our lives.

No, we did not *see* God's angels—but they were there. We thank and praise our Lord for His love and protection every step of the way.

We also thank you for reading our little story and ask you to pray with us for all the ethnic groups of Liberia who yet live and die "without Christ and without hope in this present world." Please pray that we may be able to return there to live peaceably and complete the work our Father gave us to do, and to see many come to know and love our Saviour as living Lord of their lives.

Amy:

The time my family was held in Liberia did seem long, although it was not really that long. It was pretty much a blur, but the Fry family, with whom I was living in Derby, England, were especially great. During the week I visited the Bible School in Matlock where one of the teachers said to me, "God will let you know as much as He wants you to know." That actually happened at the time Mum, Dad and Timothy were all separated from each other and I am sure it would have been much worse if I had known that, but I did not know it at the time.

Robert and Rosemarie

We were particularly grateful for those who encouraged and supported our daughter through that stressful time in her teenage years. We appreciate that her former school did not release her address to the press, who were trying to contact her for news of us. When you reflect upon what God did for her it comes down to this one thing:

He does not give us more than we can bear, Amy, Timothy or us.

Written by the Baghurst Family in the summer of 2001

Postscript: During the summer of 03 rebels forced George and Lucy to leave their home and live in the bush for about 6 weeks; by the end of the year they had returned to their home and George was endeavouring to balance his time between medical work and leadership responsibilities in his village. Please pray God will use them to build His church among the Gbloo speaking dialect of the Grebo people in southern Liberia.

The displaced must carry their homes with them

Checkpoints

Angels Everwatching

Just one among so many...

"Soldier Boy"

They arrive by the thousands in the capital

They live without God and hope in this present world…

Angels Everwatching 105

Greens and Rice – the "NPFL diet!"

"A picture is worth a thousand words!"

106   **Angels Everwatching**

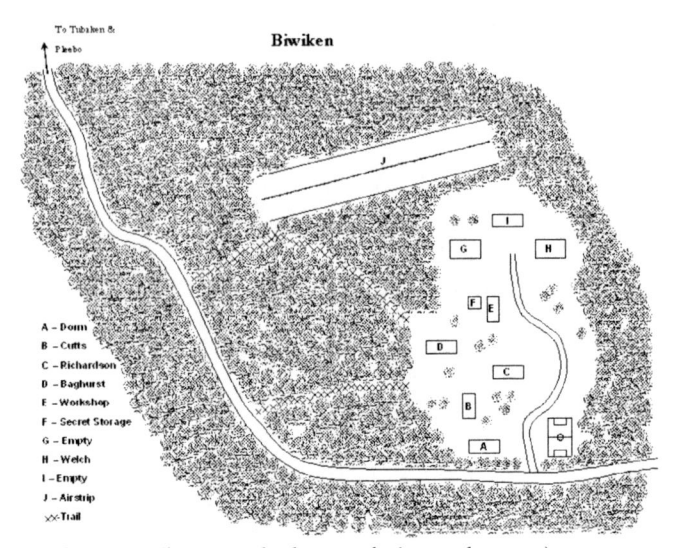

Biwiken

A – Dorm
B – Cutts
C – Richardson
D – Baghurst
E – Workshop
F – Secret Storage
G – Empty
H – Welch
I – Empty
J – Airstrip
xx- Trail

Biwiken Base (houses only shown relating to the story).

Dr. George Lott—our dear brother in Christ.

Angels Everwatching 107

George administers medication to his village people.

Harrison and Rosemary—the two eldest of the five Lott children.

The house built for the Lotts so George could run his little clinic.

Lucy cooking with daughters Rosemary, Trudy, and a village friend.

Lucy picking sweet potato greens for dinner.

Angels Everwatching 109

Lucy draws water from their hand dug well.

Their "country" kitchen.

Mother and child—precious in every culture.

The Baghurst family at the time of their first departure to Liberia. Clockwise from top, Robert, Amy, Timothy, Rosemarie.

Angels Everwatching 111

Several years later—the Baghursts in their garden.

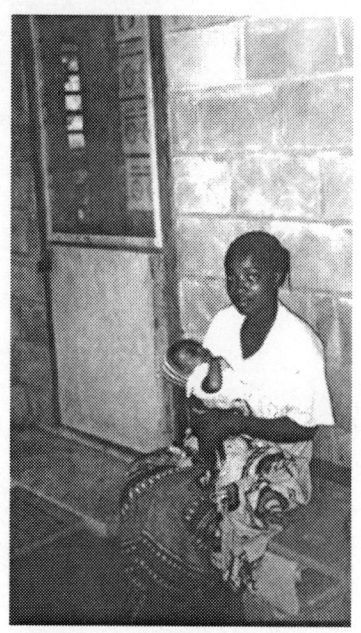

Waiting to see Dr. George.